# Investors' Preferences in Financing New Ventures

Francesco James Mazzocchini ·
Caterina Lucarelli

# Investors' Preferences in Financing New Ventures

## A Data Mining Approach to Equity

palgrave
macmillan

Francesco James Mazzocchini
Department of Management
Università Politecnica delle Marche
Ancona, Italy

Caterina Lucarelli
Department of Management
Università Politecnica delle Marche
Ancona, Italy

ISBN 978-3-031-30057-8 ISBN 978-3-031-30058-5 (eBook)
https://doi.org/10.1007/978-3-031-30058-5



This Palgrave Macmillan imprint is published by the registered company Springer Nature Switzerland AG
The registered company address is: Gewerbestrasse 11, 6330 Cham, Switzerland

# Acknowledgements

We are thankful to seminar participants of the 2022 Wolpertinger Conference in banking and finance, held at CUNEF University of Madrid (Spain), and to Federica Ielasi, Daniele Previati, Carlo Chiarella for their valuable comments and suggestions on a very preliminary version of this research.

We express also our gratitude to Emanuele Frontoni, Marco Mameli Marina Paolanti and Rocco Pietrini for their technical assistance offered in the process of the data mining and in organizing the web scraping phase.

We are also grateful to Michela Rancan for her helpful comments and suggestions at the preliminary stages of our data analysis.

# Contents

# About the Authors

**Francesco James Mazzocchini, Ph.D.,** is postdoctoral research fellow in Banking and Financial Markets at the Department of Management, Università Politecnica delle Marche, Italy. His scientific interests are in the fields of behavioural finance, investors' behaviour and decision-making under risk and uncertainty, FinTech and innovative financing, entrepreneurial finance, equity crowdfunding, blockchain and cryptoassets. In 2016, he spent one year of visiting for studying at the Innsbruck University (Austria), where he developed interest in behavioural topics. Later on, he developed a deeper understanding of the banking sector also thanks to a professional experience in an Italian financial institution in Hong Kong and Shanghai (China), before obtaining his Ph.D. *cum Laude* in Banking and Financial Markets.

**Caterina Lucarelli** is full professor of Banking and Financial Markets at the Department of Management, Università Politecnica delle Marche, Italy. Her scientific interests are in the fields of market microstructure, investors' behaviour and decision-making under risk and uncertainty, gender diversity and entrepreneurship. Since 2007, as National Coordinator of a Research Project supported by the Italian Ministry of University and Research, she has studied issues relating to individual risk tolerance, with a strict cooperation with psychologist and neuroscientists. From this experience, she has developed several research streams focusing on behaviour under risk and ambiguity, moving from financial topics (portfolio theory, investments and risk tolerance assessments) to insurance, consumers' behaviour, up to entrepreneurship and financial literacy. She now studies financial issues related to entrepreneurial talent, entrepreneurial development and new firm creation. Recently, she has been focusing on circular economy, environmental sustainability and sustainable finance.

# List of Figures

# List of Tables

CHAPTER 1

# Introduction: What Is Equity Crowdfunding and How Can the Decision-Making Process of Retail Investors Be Outlined?

**Abstract** This section reveals the content of the manuscript and introduces the work, with a short description of motivation of the research based on theories of information driving demand and supply of capital within a FinTech environment; the section underlines the additional contribution of this research, given the chance to analyse and compare a large set of equity crowdfunding platforms worldwide.

**Keywords** Entrepreneurial finance · FinTech · Equity crowdfunding · ECF platforms · Signalling theory · Observational learning theory · Herd behaviour · Information cascade · Data mining · New ventures success

Nascent entrepreneurs need to cope with money and finance, as essential to support new venture creation (among the others, Cassar, 2004). Especially when at the first stages of development, entrepreneurs face the well-known dilemmas of giving the optimal capital structure to their venture (Myers, 1984) and choosing the hierarchy of internal/external financing sources to reduce financing costs (Fazzari et al., 1988; Myers & Majluf, 1984). Nonetheless, asymmetric information inevitably affects the relation between entrepreneurs and external lenders, thus creating market frictions (Stiglitz & Weiss, 1981, 1983). Recall that transfer of funds



F. J. Mazzocchini and C. Lucarelli, *Investors' Preferences in Financing New Ventures*,
https://doi.org/10.1007/978-3-031-30058-5_1

carries with it a *struggle for information*, motivated by a very simple acknowledgement: lenders need to actively manage the risk of giving their money to entrepreneurs who may not be able to give it back, due to behaviours of adverse selection and/or moral hazard of borrowers (Stiglitz & Weiss, 1983), whatever it is the legal form of the deal.[1]

Inevitable consequence is the attempt of entrepreneurs to develop signals to effectively attract financing, being able to reduce such information asymmetries (Ahlers et al., 2015). Entrepreneurial finance necessarily entails issues related to signalling theory models as the better-informed party (entrepreneurs) need to send quality signals to the less-informed party (lenders/investors) in order to alleviate such information asymmetries (Courtney et al., 2017; Spence, 1973, 2002).

The disruptive development of technology reshaped radically this scenario of emission (and reception) of signals as vehicles of information. In the context of the financial needs of entrepreneurs, often nascent, radical innovations allowed a very large number of investors to access the financing of entrepreneurial initiatives. At first glance, one might think of a direct financial exchange model, not very different from the one achieved with Stock Exchanges, in their IPO-primary market side, where entrepreneurs ask for money to a large base of investors. Technology, nowadays, has gone *beyond* this direct exchange model, and has made it possible to implement an 'ideal' of financial democracy taken to the extreme. The partnership between Technology and Finance, which we recognize with the multifaceted expression of FinTech, has taken the meaning of 'going public' to its extreme sense. FinTech made it possible to 'go to the crowd'.

In sum, crowdfunding is a process by which a certain amount of money is raised through an open call addressed to many people, namely the 'crowd', which typically contributes modest individual amounts. Although it is commonly thought to be a recent phenomenon, crowdfunding draws its origins from the early twentieth century (e.g., the basement of the Statue of Liberty was almost entirely funded by a crowd of citizens, Harris, 1985). Thanks to the advent of the digital era and the disruptive role of FinTech, modern literature sketches various types

[1] We assume that uncertainty and risk underlying the deal between demand and supply of capital at initial steps of a venture render it comparable the position of shareholders to that one of lenders in strict sense, with a very similar effort to overcome issues of information asymmetries. This assumption renders it comparable the position of lenders (creditors) to that one of investors (shareholders).

of crowdfunding models: donation-based, reward-based, debt-based and equity crowdfunding, or also additional categories based on software-value token, commonly associated to Initial Coin Offerings (O'Dair & Owen, 2019) and litigation (Elliot, 2018).

In this research we focus on the Equity Crowdfunding (ECF), which represents a particular model of crowdfunding. Thus, crowdinvesting is the mechanism through which pre-determined amount of money is raised by a vast number of investors/backers via an open call over the Internet, allowing entrepreneurs to access to raise money. Inevitable deduction is also that crowd-investors are retail investors,[2] not particularly sophisticated in terms of financial literacy (Lukkarinen et al., 2016) and subject to the evaluation heuristic (Hsee, 1998).

Nevertheless, in this FinTech playing field and within the boundaries of ECF, a question arises: 'What about the *struggle for information?*'

The answer needs a reasoning at two stages. On the one hand, the FinTech allows the development of ECF platforms specialized in facilitating the access both of entrepreneurs in digital showcases and of crowd-investors willing to give money to ventures with 'a click of their mouse'. From this, we deduce that all the reasons behind the existence of information asymmetries necessarily here persist (Blaseg et al., 2021; Hornuf & Schwienbacher, 2018). Moreover, digital ECF platforms could render it easy, or cheap for entrepreneurs to send (quality) signals, i.e., disclosing information of themselves, of their business, with all the underling risks. Nevertheless, given for granted that entrepreneurs are willing to disclose *all* the information they possess, it stands questionable if lenders/investors, here the *crowd* of investors, can receive and decode these (quality) signals.

On the other hand, the FinTech maximizes the value of the *public* information: it is in the mandate of ECF platforms to disseminate all the information they receive, using the most transparent tool that is the Internet. At the same time, this disseminated public information can be put in storage, as well as the footprints of crowd-investors can be disclosed as objective proof of their decision-making process. Therefore, the public information disclosed by ECF platforms follows a double track: a first track is the public information related to the entrepreneur/project asking

[2] This assumption is valid through the research, nevertheless the presence of professional investors is not excluded. We set specific hypothesis for the effect of the presence of professional investors on the behaviour of retail investors.

for money, i.e., the quality signal that is emitted; the second track is the information left by the behaviours of investors, as a proof of how they received/decoded this signal and how this affected their decision-making.

In relation to this, we know from literature initially referred to trading in Stock Exchanges (Bikhchandani & Sharma, 2000; Scharfstein & Stein, 1990) that not-informed traders grab information as inferable suggestions from behaviour of the other traders, in line with what it has been suggested by the observational learning theory (Bandura & Walters, 1977). The FinTech environment, on which the ECF is based, is ideally able to facilitate this sharing of information, thanks to the mass of data and news made publicly available on the website of the ECF campaigns and updated in real time (Ahlers et al., 2015). Retail investors, therefore, can reduce information asymmetries following the simple observation of the behaviour of others (herding effect, Scharfstein & Stein, 1990), learning additional information useful to complete their decision-making framework (Schwienbacher & Larralde, 2012). The behaviour of others may ingenerate a source of information as well, generally referred as the *wisdom-of-crowds* (Polzin et al., 2017; Surowiecki, 2005). Moreover, this process, which leads to increasing the information set through the simple observation and imitation of the behaviour of more informed individuals, considered and ordered as sources, is defined as an information cascade (Bikhchandani et al., 1992; Vismara, 2018).

In this research we exploited the *public* information that FinTech maximized at the most: we regularly stored the information disclosed by ECF platforms via Internet (so by definition, *public* information) concerning, on the one hand, all the available data related to demand of money (features of the entrepreneur, the venture and the campaign). On the other hand, we stored all the available information of the supply of money, related to that campaign, with the expectation that this information can influence the decision-making of investors, as well.

Modern techniques of managing Big Data offered by Internet suggested us to adopt an innovative data mining process to collect the web data through data scraping, on a monthly basis, from a large number (ten) of ECF platforms spread worldwide, within an extended timespan (from May 2019 to October 2020). This procedure allowed us to obtain a unique dataset that has been investigated through a *hybrid* data analysis. In fact, on the one hand we followed an innovative approach to extract data and generate knowledge patterns creating data-driven models, indeed; but on the other, we tested research hypotheses, which would not be typical of data mining, adopting more traditional statistical models to uncover hidden patterns in the dataset investigating empirical evidence in line, or in contrast, with the extant literature on the field.

Furthermore, the data mining procedure based on the search and storage of all the available public information, coming from both the demand side and the offer side of the market, rendered it possible to compare various ECF platforms worldwide, with different stories and countries of origin. This allowed us to enrich the investigation of the behaviours of a further category of players involved. As we said, at a first glance the ECF exchange resembles a direct financial model, with only two players in the market, demand and supply, being entrepreneurs and investors. In the truth, this simplification is imprecise because managers of the ECF platforms, as it is going to be described in Chapter 2, are a third party in this deal, and they carry on the first screening of the project that is going to be disclosed in the web. In their entrepreneurial activity, managers of ECF platforms work as sort of financial intermediaries, put their reputation at stake when choosing to admit a given entrepreneur/project as their own ECF campaign. This offer of digital disclosure by ECF platforms becomes a business itself.

This acknowledgement reinforces the role of public information *effectively* disclosed by ECF platforms: even assuming that an entrepreneur is willing to disclose all the information available, and even assuming that managers of a given ECF platform approve to disclose this campaign, it is not given for granted that the entrepreneur's information is going to be visible in the web. One may suppose the presence of technological, or operational barriers, that might interfere with this release. Anyway, whatever is the reason for this difference in disclosing public information, we know that FinTech and the nature of digital markets per se, allow rapid and easy shifts of customers (both entrepreneurs and investors), in this case from an ECF platform to another, or also from a country to another. Therefore, in their highly competitive marketplace, the choice of ECF platform managers to enlarge, or restrict, the public information disclosed cannot be left to chance. For this reason, we presume that managers of ECF platforms are a third party in the use of public information disclosed in ECF campaigns, facing the dilemma of herding the choice of their competitors, or not. Recalling seminal studies of organizational theories (DiMaggio & Powell, 1983), thanks to our unique dataset we can investigate also if ECF platform managers followed a strategy of isomorphism, in their choice of public information disclosed.

To sum up, thanks to our dataset of the public information released by various ECF platforms worldwide, we can give answer to two research questions: first, if there is homogeneity in the sets of publicly available information displayed by ECF platforms. Secondly, what are the signals effectively learnt by retail investors, among those made publicly available, leading investors' preferences and thus bringing to success of a fundraising campaign.

To the best of our knowledge, there are no similar studies in extant literature. First, this research contributes for the methods of creating a dataset through a data-mining procedure based on grabbing the public data available in Internet. Second, we underline the innovation of our *hybrid* data analysis when we merge innovative tools, such as the creation of data-driven models, with traditional approaches of reconciling public data with hypothesis expected from extant literature. Third, this study is unique in terms of comparing the same exploratory setting against evidence shown by campaigns recorded for a large timespan and within a cross-country, cross-platform perspective. Finally, we collect information directly from the platforms' websites, assuming that this was the information set available to retail investors. This represent a further novelty if compared to extant literature because our evidence will attest if there is isomorphism in the disclosure strategy of ECF platforms, and if crowd-investors, in different countries, tend to follow similar decision-making processes.

In the remainder of this chapter, we provide a brief overview of the book's structure. Chapter 2 reviews the theoretical background upon which the study draws, recalling theories from entrepreneurial finance and corporate finance. Chapter 3 describes the data mining process adopted to gather and process the data and introduces the data analysis design. In Chapter 4, we describe the final sample obtained from data collection and provide a presentation for each of the ECF platforms investigated. Chapter 5 introduces the strategy of analysis and explains the analytical models adopted to test the research hypotheses. We also offer a review of the main findings obtained from extant literature on the field of study, which represents the benchmark for our comparison. In Chapter 6, we present and discuss the main empirical results obtained from our analyses, also through a comparison with the ones resulting from previous literature. Lastly, Chapter 7 concludes the work by offering concluding insights and some contributions to both theory and practice.

## References


Ahlers, G. K., Cumming, D., G¨unther, C., & Schweizer, D. (2015). Signaling in equity crowdfunding. *Entrepreneurship Theory and Practice, 39*(4), 955–980.

Bandura, A., & Walters, R. H. (1977). *Social learning theory* (Vol. 1). Englewood cliffs Prentice Hall.

Bikhchandani, S., Hirshleifer, D., & Welch, I. (1992). A theory of fads, fashion, custom, and cultural change as informational cascades. *Journal of Political Economy, 100*(5), 992–1026.

Bikhchandani, S., & Sharma, S. (2000). Herd behavior in financial markets. *IMF Staff Papers, 47*(3), 279–310.

Blaseg, D., Cumming, D., & Koetter, M. (2021). Equity crowdfunding: High-quality or low-quality entrepreneurs? *Entrepreneurship Theory and Practice, 45*(3), 505–530.

Cassar, G. (2004). The financing of business start-ups. *Journal of Business Venturing, 19*(2), 261–283.

Courtney, C., Dutta, S., & Li, Y. (2017). Resolving information asymmetry: Signaling, endorsement, and crowdfunding success. *Entrepreneurship Theory and Practice, 41*(2), 265–290.

DiMaggio, P. J., & Powell, W. W. (1983). The iron cage revisited: Institutional isomorphism and collective rationality in organizational fields. *American Sociological Review, 48*(2), 147–160.

Elliott, M. (2018). Trial by social media: The rise of litigation crowdfunding. *University of Cincinnati Law Review, 84*(2), 8.

Fazzari, S. M., Hubbard, R. G., & Petersen, B. C. (1988). Financing constraints and corporate investment. *Brookings Papers on Economic Activity, 1*, 141–206.

Harris, J. (1985). *A statue for America: The first 100 years of the statue of liberty*. Four Winds Press (a division of Macmillan Publishing Company). ISBN 978-0-02-742730-1.

Hornuf, L., & Schwienbacher, A. (2018). Market mechanisms and funding dynamics in equity crowdfunding. *Journal of Corporate Finance, 50*, 556–574.

Hsee, C. K. (1998). Less is better: When low-value options are valued more highly than high-value options. *Journal of Behavioral Decision Making, 11*(2), 107–121.

Lukkarinen, A., Teich, J. E., Wallenius, H., & Wallenius, J. (2016). Success drivers of online equity crowdfunding campaigns. *Decision Support Systems, 87*, 26–38.

Myers, S. C. (1984). The capital structure puzzle. *Journal of Finance, 39*, 575–592.

Myers, S. C., & Majluf, N. (1984). Corporate financing and investment decisions when firms have information that investors do not have. *Journal of Financial Economics, 13*, 187–221.

O'Dair, M., & Owen, R. (2019). Financing new creative enterprise through blockchain technology: Opportunities and policy implications. *Strategic Change, 28*(1), 9–17.

Polzin, F., Toxopeus, H., & Stam, E. (2017). The wisdom of the crowd in funding: Information heterogeneity and social networks of crowdfunders. *Small Business Economics, 50*, 251–273.

Scharfstein, D. S., & Stein, J. C. (1990). Herd behavior and investment. *The American Economic Review, 80*, 465–479.

Schwienbacher, A., & Larralde, B. (2012). Alternative types of entrepreneurial finance.

Spence, M. (1973). Job market signaling. *The Quarterly Journal of Economics, 87*(3), 355–374.

Spence, M. (2002). Signaling in retrospect and the informational structure of markets. *American Economic Review, 92*(3), 434–459.

Stiglitz, J. E., & Weiss, A. (1981). Credit rationing in markets with imperfect information. *The American Economic Review, 71*(3), 393–410.

Stiglitz, J., & Weiss, A. (1983). Alternative approaches to analyzing markets with asymmetric information: Reply. *The American Economic Review, 73*(1), 246–249.

Surowiecki, J. (2005). *The wisdom of crowds*. Anchor Books.

Vismara, S. (2018). Information cascades among investors in equity crowdfunding. *Entrepreneurship Theory and Practice, 42*(3), 467–497.

CHAPTER 2

# About Entrepreneurial Finance and Factors Affecting Crowd-Investor Preferences

**Abstract** This section lays the ground and reviews the literature upon which the work draws. On one hand, the theoretical background is based on the entrepreneurial finance pillar, which studies the FinTech environment and, in particular, the crowdfunding phenomenon. On the other hand, the framework comprises theories about information asymmetry and signalling. The intersection of the two leads to the literature on the crowd-investors' preferences and drivers for conducting a successful equity crowdfunding campaign. The section ends with the development of the research question and hypotheses.

**Keywords** Entrepreneurial finance · Pecking order · FinTech · Equity crowdfunding · Information asymmetry · Signalling · Crowdinvesting · Institutional isomorphism · Information dissemination

## 2.1 Entrepreneurial Finance

At the very first stage and before beginning the business cycle, prospective entrepreneurs commonly face the main challenge of finding adequate financial resources to commercialize their business ideas. The first step concerns the financial planning, where founders have to estimate both the



F. J. Mazzocchini and C. Lucarelli, *Investors' Preferences in Financing New Ventures*,
https://doi.org/10.1007/978-3-031-30058-5_2

amount of capital needed and its timing. In this phase, it is of the essence to understand the financial needs of the new venture and strategically anticipate future cash needs.

The venture's preference towards its capital structure is explained by two main theories: the static Trade-off Theory and the Pecking Order Theory. The former was developed from Modigliani and Miller (1958) to investigate the hypothetical existence of an optimal capital structure able to maximize the market value of a venture. The theory states that in efficient markets and under a series of explicit and implicit assumptions, the capital structure of a venture is irrelevant as its market value is not affected by the use of leverage but rather from investment earnings (Modigliani & Miller, 1958).

The latter theory suggests that ventures adhere to a hierarchy of financing sources and prioritize internal funds to external ones (Myers & Majluf, 1984), in order to reduce financing costs. The reason is that the costs increase with asymmetric information between entrepreneurs and prospective shareholders. As opposed to the Trade-off Theory, the Pecking Order Theory would explain the reason for which leverage might appear lower for more profitable firms (Fazzari et al., 1988; Myers, 1984). These two theories were developed within the corporate finance framework and thus originally applied to more mature firms. However, literature considers the pecking order theory relevant also within the entrepreneurial finance framework (Cosh et al., 2009).

According to the pecking order theory, first new ventures' founders bring in own capital (i.e., self-financing), which is immune from information asymmetry and less prone to risks by definition. Commonly, own capital for startups consists primarily of insider finance, i.e., money from the founders and/or their relatives.

However, the launch of a new venture usually requires a large amount of capital. Unless founders are able to provide enough owner financing, they need to source external contributors willing to fund their concepts. Among the external financing methods, once that internal funds are depleted, entrepreneurs first prefer to opt for debt in the forms of either business debt or personal debt (Cole & Sokolyk, 2018). Business debt comprises debt borrowed from financial institutions (e.g., bank financing), from the market (e.g., bonds) and from business suppliers (e.g., trade credit). Bank financing is usually based on business loans, which require a pledged asset (i.e., collateral) to secure the repayments and are granted after a strict evaluation process. Financial institution financing includes also microloans, asset-based financing, invoice financing, business cash advances, cash flow loans and mezzanine financing. In addition, entrepreneurs might originate debt from the market by issuing bonds, which are debt instruments under which the holders (creditors) are entitled to receive cash flows (i.e., interests and principal amount borrowed) from the borrower (e.g., the firm) over a specified period until the maturity date. The most common procedure is called underwriting and requires the support of a financial institution that acts as the underwriter. Business suppliers financing methods consider mainly trade credit and promissory notes (mostly for mature firms).

Lastly, when it is not feasible to incur more debt, new equity is issued. Equity comprises the offering of securities (e.g., through an Initial Public Offering) or the participation of external investors to the share capital that may come in the forms of angel investment, venture capital, crowdinvesting and other alternative financial channels. Angel investment consists of a private investor (business angel) who confers her own capital and technical or managerial support to new ventures in exchange for ownership shares. Business angels commonly bear high risks by investing their own capital in innovative startups at their seeding stages (seed capital). However, the expected returns on investment for those (few) startups that reach later stages (growth phase) are equally high. Unlike angel investment, venture capital invests a pooled amount of capital raised in the form of funds from investors (Limited Partners; e.g., high-net-worth private investors, hedge funds, pension funds, investment banks, insurance companies and other financial institutions). Crowdinvesting is the mechanism through which pre-determined amount of money is raised from a vast number of investors/backers via an open call over the internet.

In general, debt is preferred over new equity to avoid the increasing costs related to the entrance of external ownership into the company. For this reason, equity stands lower in the hierarchy of the financing sources and, according to the pecking order theory, it is considered as a last resort. This holds particularly true for new ventures and SMEs, as they commonly prefer the less-burdening method in terms of information disclosure.

## 2.2 FinTech and Equity Crowdfunding

Lately, the financial system has experienced an increasing and ongoing usage of innovative and technological tools to compete with traditional financial methods. This revolution is commonly known with the term ‘FinTech’, a *crasis* for ‘Financial Technology’, and started to be widespread since around 2014. It consists of a superstructure that comprises different technologies, platforms and tools to support traditional financial services. It offers indeed a wide range of digital solutions (Lee & Shin, 2018; Ma & Liu, 2017), including among all: digital payments and transactions, Peer-to-peer (P2P) lending, crowdfunding (CF), cryptocurrencies, cloud computing, wealth management, Robotic Process Automation (RPA), Robo-advisory, Artificial Intelligence (AI), Machine Learning (ML), InsurTech, Big Data management and analytics, distributed ledger technologies (DLT), traceable blockchain processes and smart contracts.

This book focuses on one FinTech activity in particular: the equity crowdfunding (ECF), which represents a particular model of crowdfunding. In general, crowdfunding is a financing mechanism that allows a plethora of individuals to back monetarily a project (i.e., fundraising campaign) through a digital platform over the internet. The modern crowdfunding practice distinguishes three main categories of models: philanthropic based, non-financial-returns based and financial-returns based. To the first category belongs the donation crowdfunding, which is a popular type of crowdfunding where individuals back charitable causes (e.g., socio environmental, religious or other purposes). Their joint effort is free and not motivated by any direct return but rather by intangible rewards such as altruism, peer recognition, respect or esteem (Choy & Schlagwein, 2016). Mollick (2014) defines it also as patronage model. The second category comprises the reward-based crowdfunding that, together with the donation based, is one of the oldest crowdfunding practices. Bids are made with the expectation of a non-financial returns, namely the reward, which consists of the delivery at a later date of a giveaway or a pre-sell of the product that will appear on the market if the fundraising target is met and the business takes off (‘pre-ordering crowdfunding’; Belleflamme et al., 2014). The third category is the broadest one and includes, among other models: the debt-based, digital-security based, litigation-based and equity-based crowdfunding. Debt-based crowdfunding, known also as lending or peer-to-peer model, consists of a loan granted by the crowd of backers with the expectation of obtaining the principal plus some interests in return. Digital-security based crowdfunding offers software-value tokens (a quantity of cryptocurrency coins) as a reward to backers that funds the project (O’Dair & Owen, 2019). If the funding target is met and the project takes off, the tokens will serve as functional units of currency. The process is known as Initial Coin Offering (ICO). Litigation crowdfunding funds legal actions of plaintiffs or defendants with peer's money. Backers purchase a stake in a claim and, if the case succeeds or is settled, they obtain a monetary reward (Elliott, 2018), according to the ultimate compensation obtained by the litigant at the end of the lawsuit (i.e., *pactum de quota litis*: a contingent or success fee). Equity-based crowdfunding is more sophisticated than the previous models for both the issuer and the backer (investor) in that it involves the participation of the latter in ownership stakes of a company. For this reason, it is also subject to stricter and increasing regulations (Heminway & Hoffman, 2010) from governmental authorities. The issuer, generally an innovative new venture, offers equity shares of its equity in return for funding capital. If the fundraising target is met, the fundraising campaign is successful and the crowd of investors turn into shareholders. Due to its financial-return-based nature, ECF is also defined as 'profit sharing crowdfunding' (Belleflamme et al., 2014).

Previous literature investigated whether ECF should represent a first resort for new ventures, and thus the pecking order should be reversed (Fulghieri et al., 2014), or a last resort (i.e., it stands lower in the pecking order hierarchy among the equity alternatives). The prevalence of literature positions it as a last resort financing mechanism to seek when internal funds and debt capacity are depleted (Walthoff-Borm et al., 2018).

## 2.3 Information Asymmetry and Signalling Theory

Seeking seed financing represents an outstanding issue for founders (Eckhardt et al., 2006), especially in contexts of asymmetric information. On one hand, they hardly possess sufficient own capital. On the other hand, they might face bank credit rationing and lack basic requirements for bond or stock issue (Kirby & Worner, 2014). Indeed, asymmetric information between entrepreneurs and stakeholders is ineluctable (Cassar, 2004) and might lead to a suboptimal allocation of resources and market frictions (Stiglitz & Weiss, 1981, 1983). It drives financing costs up due to the exposure to risks associated with the business and, as a consequence, financing sources require higher returns. In this situation, ECF might represent a valid alternative to raise financing. Belonging to the FinTech environment (Blaseg et al., 2021), it represents a digital finance mechanism that allows real-time information updates and ease information sharing through the platforms' websites and access to social media networks. However, in order to attract investors and money, entrepreneurs are still required to establish trust-based stakeholder relationships (Pollack et al., 2017).

In other words, observing the phenomenon through the lenses of contract theory, and more specifically agency theory, information asymmetries originate agency costs (Jensen & Meckling, 1976), which are costs deriving from contractual arrangements under imperfect information between two parties (i.e., a principal and an agent). Applying the principal-agent frame to the ECF context, the agents (the founders) possess wider private information about the quality/risks of the business project than the principals (crowd-investors). The inability of the principals to discern between high-quality and low-quality business projects—undertaken by agents—might lead to adverse selection and moral hazard issues (Akerlof, 1970; Carpenter & Petersen, 2002). Therefore, entrepreneurs are required to convey quality signals to stakeholders in order to develop dimensions of trust and effectively attract financing (Ahlers et al., 2015; Courtney et al., 2017; Pollack et al., 2017).

As a matter of fact, signalling theory models a situation within the contract theory framework in which the better-informed party is able to send quality signals to the less-informed party to alleviate information asymmetries (Spence, 1973, 2002). In his seminal article, Spence (1973) first developed the theory in which a signalling model was initially applied to the job market, where employers are not able to observe intangible traits of job seekers and face an investment (hiring) under uncertainty. Employees can use/acquire education credentials to convey effective signals to reduce employers' information deficit. Since the seminal article, signalling theory has been extended to different fields in economics and business studies (Connelly et al., 2011), such as entrepreneurship, without varying the key elements. In particular, Leland and Pyle (1977) applied the theory to the Initial Public Offering (IPO) process, where high-quality companies are required to send clear signals to the market in order to prevent adverse selection. Similarly, the model can be applied to the ECF context, which is comparable to an IPO in several respects.

The signalling procedure is typically based on three steps: (i) the information insider (signaller) conveys private or intangible information in her possession to alleviate information asymmetries, (ii) the information outsider (receiver) observes and interprets the signal and (iii) the receiver eventually makes a decision based on the signal and feedback is sent to the signaller (Block et al., 2018; Connelly et al., 2011). The main assumption is that the signal should be reliable. In other words, it should not be effortlessly imitated by low-quality companies in order to prevent moral hazard issues. However, a recent study from Johan and Zhang (2020) suggests a revisit of the traditional signalling theory. The authors claim that in presence of an unsophisticated audience—i.e., in the ECF context—less costly signals facilitate communication between entrepreneurs and crowd-investors.

## 2.4 The Actors in the Process

There are several actors involved in the ECF landscape: (i) entrepreneurs, (ii) investors, (iii) managers of platforms, (iv) advisors and (v) regulators.

Entrepreneurs are commonly the founders of the new venture and the initiators of the fundraising campaign. They require additional funding to start or expand their business and, weighing up all the options, they opt for this financing source. They start the process by choosing the crowdfunding model and platform. Then, they set out the details (e.g., duration, share price, shares of equity retained, funding targets, etc.) of the fundraising campaign thanks also to the support provided by advisors. It is crucial that the funding targets are set effectively. In particular, entrepreneurs are required to specify both a minimum fundraising target and a maximum fundraising target. The former usually represents the necessary amount of funding needed by the new venture and, once reached, it defines the success of the campaign. The latter represents the upper bound (i.e., cap) of investments accepted, in order to limit the excessive equity dilution. Indeed, funding targets are calculated depending on the value of equity and on the percentage of shares that entrepreneurs consider appropriate to offer to new shareholders. On the flipside, it also defines the shares of equity that is retained by entrepreneurs after the offering. Therefore, reaching the maximum target—i.e., the campaign is overfunding as it exceeds the minimum target—entails the immediate successful conclusion of the campaign. Once the investment details are finalized, they file for getting accepted by the platform. If accepted, they are required to prepare the pitch phase in which they describe the business idea, the purpose of funding, and promote the project to attract prospective investors.

Investors provide the necessary funding to entrepreneurs and obtain equity shares in return, thus participating to the venture capital of the new venture. They are registered members (i.e., accredited as investors) of the digital platform where the fundraising campaign is launched. Browsing the platform website, they are able to scroll the open fundraising campaigns to evaluate the investment opportunities. Once they pick the project that they consider most promising, they bid for one or more shares. The investment is then finalized as soon as the payment is confirmed. The last step is not insignificant as literature found out that non-confirmed bids might be used as an information manipulation tool to attract late investors (Meoli & Vismara, 2021).

Investors can be distinguished into retail investors and professional investors. The former are ordinary people that usually invest small amounts of money and rarely possess investment experience or financial expertise. The latter, instead, are sophisticated investors with both investment experience and financial expertise that invest larger amounts of money. Professional investors usually coincide with institutional investors and include financial institutions, investment banks, funds and hedge funds, venture capital firm, business angels, high-net-worth individuals and other large corporations. The pool of investors that back an ECF campaign is commonly known as the crowd of investors.

ECF platforms are digital portals that facilitate the matching of demand (i.e., entrepreneurs) and supply (i.e., crowd of investors) for capital on the web. They not only host fundraising campaigns on their website, but also carry out several important tasks. Once a project is presented to an ECF platform for acceptance, platform managers conduct a pre-screening phase in which the project and the firm are evaluated. The evaluation is based on due diligence check and on the examination of the business idea, business plan and entrepreneurial team (Kleinert & Volkmann, 2019). Eventually, if the verdict is favourable, platform managers decide to launch the fundraising campaign on their website for an arranged time frame. Typically, 90% of the projects do not pass the pre-screening phase (Kleinert & Volkmann, 2019). Besides that, platform managers provide support and intermediate between entrepreneurs and the market (i.e., the crowd of investors). In particular, thanks also to the digital nature of the process (i.e., FinTech), ECF platforms ease information sharing and offer a wide set of transparent information and live updates about the campaign and the projects to the investing audience. ECF platforms are, definitively, business organizations that earn money through fees for their services.

Advisors provide initial support to entrepreneurs in order to effectively design the fundraising campaign and present the business idea, as well as expand the entrepreneurial network by connecting them to new potential stakeholders. They might also possess digital marketing expertise and support its promotion, advertising and communication with the audience.

Regulators (i.e., securities regulatory authorities) are governmental agencies that regulate investment services and operations. Their aim is to ensure transparency, safeguard investors and prevent frauds and unfair conducts.

## 2.5 Platforms' Isomorphism

In free market, ECF platforms act as business entities and compete against each other to generate profits (Jullien & Sand-Zantman, 2020). On one hand, competition might induce imitation practices and convergence (i.e., catching up) between the platforms, leading to homogeneity of organizational forms and practices. On the other hand, it explains why heterogeneity among platforms can be observed, especially at initial stages of their life cycle.

In sociological literature, the homogenization phenomenon between business organizations is defined as institutional isomorphism (DiMaggio & Powell, 1983). Indeed, organizational theory describes isomorphism as the process of imitating or resembling the structure of other organizations under the same environmental circumstances (i.e., *ceteris paribus*). The authors identify three main types: mimetic, coercive and normative. Mimetic isomorphism refers to the imitation process of the structure and behaviour of a more successful organization in the field, which is considered the role model. Being induced by uncertainty and lack of more suitable organizational procedures, it represents a deliberate mimicking behaviour that is encouraged by internal forces.

Coercive isomorphism, instead, refers to the homogenization process induced by external organizations, which can be formal (e.g., governmental mandates, regulators) or informal (e.g., cultural expectations, society and other linked organizations). The result is the adoption of standardized procedures and behaviours among organizations operating in a common environment.

Like coercive isomorphism, normative isomorphism is induced by external forces. Indeed, it can be generated by groups of professionals—i.e., professional networks—that define methods and professional behaviours, leading ultimately to the creation of professional standards.

## 2.6 Drivers for the Crowd-Investors' Action and Preferences

Success in ECF might be analyzed from three different perspectives and refer to different stages in the process: ex-ante success, campaign success and post-offering success. The former concept refers to the pre-screening phase in which a campaign is presented to a platform for acceptance. If the evaluation of platform managers concludes successfully, the venture is admitted for listing. Before going live, the campaigns have the opportunity to launch a private funding stage open only to families, friends and platform managers. The rationale for this soft-launch is to boost the likelihood of closing the subsequent public round successfully by enhancing the crowd confidence through a head-start. The latter success perspective—i.e., post-offering success—refers to the ability of the funded venture to generate value and grow in the medium-long term—i.e., enter and remain in the market, produce appreciable cash flows and reach a more mature stage. Instead, the second (intermediate) stage of success refers to the campaign success and is the only success perspective on which this study is focused.

Once a fundraising campaign is launched, it will be live on the platform's website and open for investments for a specific time frame. Recalling that the campaign closes either when the time is up or as soon as it reaches the maximum funding target, both the investing time left and the percentage of funding raised (i.e., amount of capital raised in relation to the minimum target) up to that moment are displayed on the headings of its webpage.

Therefore, the success of an ECF campaign is driven by investment decisions made by the crowd of investors. On the other side of the coin, entrepreneurs are required to leverage the main features of their project in order to promote their business idea and make it more appealing to prospective investors. In this regard, signalling strategies support entrepreneurs to match investors' preferences and ultimately attract capital.

Literature argues that the influence of entrepreneurs on the preferences of investors and financing sources is particularly pronounced for new ventures and smaller firms (Cassar, 2004). Among all, entrepreneurs' traits and entrepreneurs' risk appetite can represent signals of the project viability.

A branch of ECF literature investigated the main factors that influence investors' preferences and drive investment decisions. However, the factors are often analysed in isolation and literature may sometimes appear

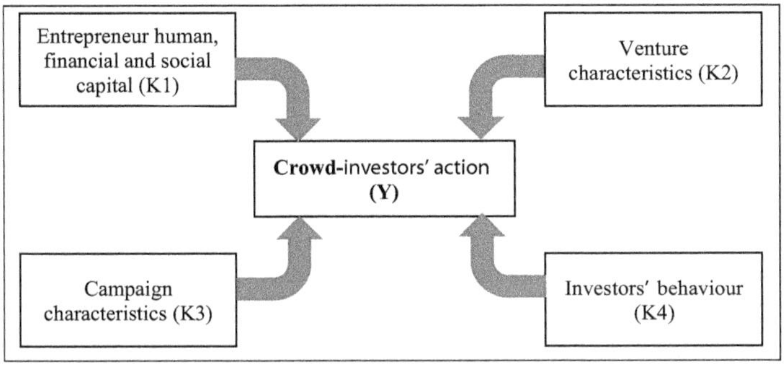


**Fig. 2.1** Drivers for the Crowd-investors' action

fragmentary. In this book, we offer a new perspective on drivers for investment actions of the crowd, starting from the main findings obtained separately by previous literature. We create a theoretical model based on four groups of variables, already proposed by literature (Fig. 2.1): (i) human, financial and social capital of entrepreneurs, (ii) new venture characteristics, (iii) campaign characteristics and (iv) investors' behaviour.

### *2.6.1 Entrepreneur Financial, Human and Social Capital (K1)*

The former category, namely the K1 group, relates to the entrepreneurs' characteristics and includes their traits, financial commitment and risk appetite, human capital and social capital. Literature considers these features as effective signals of quality of a business project, especially at its seeding stages (Cassar, 2004).

The composition of the entrepreneurial team and its traits—e.g., age, gender and experience—are all signals of the quality of a project in terms of effort, competence and reliability (i.e., human capital).

Similarly, entrepreneurs, as information insiders, are able to convey signals about their own commitment and self-confidence in their business ideas. Their financial commitment, which is represented both by the amount of own capital contribution and the share of equity retained, is an effective signal of their skin-in-the-game (Frid et al., 2015) and risk appetite. Indeed, entrepreneurs' willingness to bear the risks of their own project represents a positive signal and is revealed by the share of equity retained (Leland & Pyle, 1977; Löher et al., 2018; Vismara, 2016).

A less informative but still effective signal is represented by the social capital of entrepreneurs, expressed in terms of social media network. Given the digital nature of the phenomenon, social media represent information hubs (Vrontis et al., 2021). They are crucial not only for business promotion and knowledge sharing but also for expanding the entrepreneurs' social network (i.e., social capital) and connecting with potential stakeholders. Following previous studies, the online presence of entrepreneurs acts as an endorsement of project quality (Barbi & Mattioli, 2019; Vismara, 2016). Indeed, social media provide access to project updates and discussions and enable interactions between investors and founders.

### 2.6.2 *Venture Characteristics (K2)*

Venture's characteristics represent another set of signals, namely the group K2, that define the viability of the business project for which entrepreneurs are raising funds. The category includes size, maturity, location, asset structure, business evaluation, growth opportunities, financial figures and other quantitative business information.

Following previous studies, crowd-investors prefer to invest locally (Agrawal et al., 2015), as they are more familiar with the country and the market in which the new venture is going to compete, recalling familiarity and home biases. Indeed, geographical proximity reduces screening costs, improves project selection and eases due diligence and monitoring processes (Vrontis et al., 2021). Moreover, according to the cultural dimensions' theory (Hofstede, 2011), differences in culture across countries affect the values and behaviours of their members.

Literature also suggests that investors in ECF, in contrast to non-equity-based crowdfunding, are financially motivated and pay attention to information about business potentials (Löher et al., 2018). The pre-money valuation provides an estimate of the value of the new venture before raising funds. The information is reported by the entrepreneur herself on the campaign webpage, but it is evaluated by experts such as advisors or analysts who have access to a wider set of information and skills than investors; they can also possibly observe softer pieces of information about the entrepreneurial team and entrepreneurs themselves, as they cooperate with them to aggregate useful information in order to produce an objective pre-money valuation. In line with literature on financially motivated financing behaviour, crowd-investors attempt to reduce information asymmetries by picking projects with higher valuations as positive signals conveyed by better-informed parties (Löher et al., 2018).

However, recent literature found that retail investors tend to pay scarce attention to sophisticated (i.e., costly) signals—i.e., financial information and metrics—due to perceived difficulty to understand it (Johan & Zhang, 2020; Shafi, 2021).

### *2.6.3 Campaign Characteristics (K3)*

Campaign's characteristics, here the group K3, define the investment details and funding round characteristics that have been set by the entrepreneurs with the support of advisors prior to the offering (i.e., share price, minimum funding target and maximum funding target).

The share price is often presented by platforms as the minimum investment amount—i.e., the denominated value. Although not extensively studied in the literature, higher prices appear to discourage retail investors from taking investment risks (Lukkarinen et al., 2016).

Similarly, higher funding targets seem to be less appealing for investors and are negatively related to campaign success (Ralcheva & Roosenboom, 2020; Vulkan et al., 2016).

To these features, we also included campaign-specific characteristics, such as a dummy variable that denotes whether the fundraising campaign was launched after the COVID-19 pandemic. It is an unprecedented variable that has not yet been investigated in ECF literature. However recent studies appear unanimous in claiming that the pandemic has fostered the usage of FinTech (Fu & Mishra, 2022; Le, 2021).

### *2.6.4 Investors' Behaviour (K4/Y)*

Investors' behaviour, here the group K4, refers to the set of signals that the crowd conveys to prospective and undecided investors. In this regard, signals come from the number of investors that already financed the project, the amount/percentage of capital that they have actually conferred (i.e., financial commitment), the number of followers of the campaign (i.e., prospective investors who 'liked' the campaign and follow its updates) and the presence of professional investors.

The observational learning theory, also known as social learning theory (Bandura & Walters, 1977), predicts that individuals tend to rely on the decision-making of better-informed parties, when facing imperfect information (Bikhchandani & Sharma, 2000). According to this theory, late investors are able to learn from the behaviour of better-informed economic agents (i.e., early investors, professional investors) and thus downscale asymmetric information. The investors' attitude to imitate the behaviour of others is commonly known within social finance studies as herding or herd behaviour (Bikhchandani & Sharma, 2000; Scharfstein & Stein, 1990).

Indeed, platforms transparently show the number, amount, proportion, frequency and timing of bids made by both unqualified and qualified investors. A precise and easily understandable indicator of the early bids made is the percentage of target amount raised, which, eventually, represents a weighted measure of the financial engagement of external shareholders. Similarly, the number of bids made could represent an effective signal that can be utilized as additional source of information to evaluate the quality of a campaign, and thus business potential (Kleinert & Volkmann, 2019; Löher et al., 2018).

Previous literature has shown that early investments can effectively increase the likelihood of success by attracting crowd-investors via information cascades (Hornuf & Schwienbacher, 2018; Vismara, 2018), as late bidders are more prone to invest in a project that is about to conclude successfully (Scharfstein & Stein, 1990).

The investment behaviour of experts is another publicly available source of information that reveals whether sophisticated investors or qualified investors with higher financial capabilities and expertise and/or investment institutions support the project, often with larger bids. Their presence is seen as a good quality signal by crowd-investors, who presume that professional investors have access to wider information sets. At the same time, the presence of qualified investors extends beyond financial aspects, as they provide a wider set of value-added services to the new venture (Signori & Vismara, 2018). Thus, the investments made by qualified investors attract late investors by both acting as a certification effect on business potential and reflecting a positive outlook.

However, it is also believed that the wisdom of the crowd, collectively, can outperform the expertise and capabilities of individual experts (Surowiecki, 2005), as a signal regarding the good outlook of the investment (Block et al., 2018). This explains why prospective crowd-investors engage in active observational learning (rational herding) from peers (Zhang & Liu, 2012).

As a consequence, this last basket of signals contains inevitably both explanatory variables and dependent variables of our forthcoming theoretical model and econometric estimates.

## 2.7 Research Questions and Research Hypotheses

The research design applies the signalling theory and social learning theory to the ECF environment, where investors have access to a wide set of information on the aforementioned four categories of drivers. In particular, we aim at retracing the investment path—i.e., investor experience—of concluded campaigns filling the shoes of a retail investor. Assuming her perspective, we observe the scenario—i.e., information set—that is available to her before finalizing an investment decision.

Previous literature on the topic analyzed factors affecting the success of a campaign in isolation and mainly creating a dataset of private information provided by ECF platforms. In this study, we collect information directly from the platforms' websites—i.e., publicly available information—starting from the assumption that it depicts the information set available to retail investors. Here lies the main novelty of this study if compared to extant literature.

Applying the theory to the organizational structure of ECF platforms, we might observe structural homogenizations among them. In other words, we might expect that a platform tends to resemble another platform that face the same environmental conditions, thus offering similar webpage layouts and, most importantly, comparable sets of public information about the campaigns.

Based on the theoretical framework, the study first aims to answer the following research question:

> ***RQ1:*** Is there homogeneity in the sets of publicly available information displayed by ECF platforms?

Investors' preferences are crucial to ensure financing of new ventures. Definitively, investors' choices determine the success of a fundraising campaign. Dimensions of this success are variegated. On one hand it could simply measure whether the amount of money requested has been raised, ending up being a *yes*, enough money, or *not*. Differently, we could also aim at examining different nuances of success, in terms of percentage of funding obtained in relation to the desired amount, amount of capital actually raised (i.e., regardless of the aimed target), number of investors financially committed to the project (i.e., even if with smaller amount/denominations) and presence of professional investors (Table 2.1).

**Table 2.1** Metrics of campaign success (dependent variables)

| | | |
|---|---|---|
| Success | Campaign success (dichotomous)—i.e., minimum funding target is reached | Y1 |
| Percentage raised | Percentage of funding raised in relation to minimum funding target | Y2 |
| Capital raised | Amount of capital raised (in €) | Y3 |
| Number of investors | Extension of the crowd: sum of both retail and professional investors | Y4 |
| Professional investors | Presence of professional investors (i.e., institutional and sophisticated investors) | Y5 |

**Fig. 2.2** Theoretical model

It follows the second research question of this study.

> ***RQ2:*** What are the signals effectively learnt by prospective retail investors, among those made publicly available by equity crowdfunding platforms, that can affect investors' preferences and thus success of a fundraising campaign?

Based on the research questions, we develop a theoretical model (Fig. 2.2) where the research hypotheses are incorporated into the four categories of drivers: entrepreneurs' characteristics, venture characteristics, campaign round characteristics and crowd's behaviour.

Following the theoretical model and the literature on drivers of crowd-investors' action, research hypotheses are then specified as follows (Table 2.2).

**Table 2.2** Research hypotheses

| *Category* | *Driver* | *RH#* | *Research hypotheses* |
|---|---|---|---|
| Entrepreneur's human, financial and social capital (K1) | Human capital | H1 | Human capital of entrepreneurs influences the likelihood of getting funded, with different sign of the relationship (De Crescenzo et al., 2020; Nitani et al., 2019; Ralcheva & Roosenboom, 2020) |
| | Financial commitment | H2 | Entrepreneurs' financial commitment influences the odds of being finances, but alternative expectations are admitted (positive—i.e., a larger stake of equity retained—Leland & Pyle, 1977; Löher et al., 2018; Vismara, 2016; or negative due to sign of overconfidence—Singh, 2020) |
| | Social capital | H3 | The presence of entrepreneurs/new ventures on social media networks—i.e., social capital— increases the likelihood of getting funded (Vismara, 2016; Vrontis et al., 2021) |
| Venture characteristics (K2) | Financial forecast | H4 | Ventures capable of generating revenues—i.e., financial metrics and financial forecasts—have more probabilities of getting funded (Ahlers et al., 2015; Nitani et al., 2019) |
| | Pre-money | H5 | Higher pre-money as business evaluations influences the likelihood of getting funded but alternative expectations are admitted (positive as in Löher et al., 2018; negative as in Coakley et al., 2022) |

(continued)

**Table 2.2** (continued)

| *Category* | *Driver* | *RH#* | *Research hypotheses* |
|---|---|---|---|
| | Firm location | H6 | Domestic ventures are more likely to get funded (Agrawal et al., 2015), but non-significant relationships are admitted (Coakley et al., 2022; Shafi, 2021) |
| | Firm maturity | H7 | Enterprise business age increases the likelihood of getting funded (Li et al., 2016) |
| Campaign characteristics (K3) | Share price | H8 | Lower prices per share increase the likelihood of getting funded (Lukkarinen et al., 2016) |
| | Min funding target | H9 | Lower funding targets increase the likelihood of getting funded (Ralcheva & Roosenboom, 2020; Vulkan et al., 2016) |
| Investors' behaviour (K4) | Investors commitment | H10 | The investors' commitment—i.e., interest showed in terms of effective investments—positively impacts the likelihood of getting funded (Hornuf & Schwienbacher, 2018) |
| | Investors' presence | H11 | A higher number of crowd-investors increase the likelihood getting funded, reflecting the wisdom of the crowd (Surowiecki, 2005; Zhang & Liu, 2012) |
| | Professional investors | H12 | The presence of professional investors increases the likelihood of getting funded (Löher et al., 2018) |

## References

Agrawal, A., Catalini, C., & Goldfarb, A. (2015). Crowdfunding: Geography, social networks, and the timing of investment decisions. *Journal of Economics & Management Strategy, 24*(2), 253–274.

Ahlers, G. K., Cumming, D., Günther, C., & Schweizer, D. (2015). Signaling in equity crowdfunding. *Entrepreneurship Theory and Practice, 39*(4), 955–980.

Akerlof, G. (1970). The market for "lemons": Quality uncertainty and the market mechanism. *Quarterly Journal of Economics, 84*(3), 488–500.

Bandura, A., & Walters, R. H. (1977). *Social learning theory* (Vol. 1). Englewood cliffs Prentice Hall.

Barbi, M., & Mattioli, S. (2019). Human capital, investor trust, and equity crowdfunding. *Research in International Business and Finance, 49*, 1–12.

Belleflamme, P., Lambert, T., & Schwienbacher, A. (2014). Crowdfunding: Tapping the right crowd. *Journal of Business Venturing*, *29*(5), 585–609. https://doi.org/10.1016/j.jbusvent.2013.07.003

Bikhchandani, S., & Sharma, S. (2000). Herd behavior in financial markets. *IMF Staff Papers, 47*(3), 279–310.

Blaseg, D., Cumming, D., & Koetter, M. (2021). Equity crowdfunding: High-quality or low-quality entrepreneurs? *Entrepreneurship Theory and Practice, 45*(3), 505–530.

Block, J. H., Colombo, M. G., Cumming, D.J., & Vismara, S. (2018). New players in entrepreneurial finance and why they are there. *Small Business Economics, 50*(2), 239–250. https://doi.org/10.1007/s11187-016-9826-6

Carpenter, R. E., & Petersen, B. C. (2002). Capital market imperfections, high-tech investment, and new equity financing. *The Economic Journal, 112*(477), F54–F72.

Cassar, G. (2004). The financing of business start-ups. *Journal of Business Venturing, 19*(2), 261–283.

Choy, K., & Schlagwein, D. (2016). Crowdsourcing for a better world: On the relation between IT affordances and donor motivations in charitable crowdfunding. *Information Technology & People, 29*(1), 221–247. https://doi.org/10.1108/ITP-09-2014-0215

Coakley, J., Lazos, A., & Liñares-Zegarra, J. M. (2022). Equity crowdfunding founder teams: Campaign success and venture failure. *British Journal of Management*, *33*(1), 286–305.

Cole, R. A., & Sokolyk, T. (2018). Debt financing, survival, and growth of start-up firms. *Journal of Corporate Finance, 50*, 609–625. ISSN 0929-1199. https://doi.org/10.1016/j.jcorpfin.2017.10.013

Connelly, B. L., Certo, S. T., Ireland, R. D., & Reutzel, C. R. (2011). Signaling theory: A review and assessment. *Journal of Management, 37*(1), 39–67.

Cosh, A., Cumming, D., & Hughes, A. (2009). Outside enterpreneurial capital. *The Economic Journal, 119*(540), 1494–1533. https://doi.org/10.1111/j.1468-0297.2009.02270.x

Courtney, C., Dutta, S., & Li, Y. (2017). Resolving information asymmetry: Signaling, endorsement, and crowdfunding success. *Entrepreneurship Theory and Practice, 41*(2), 265–290.

De Crescenzo, V., Ribeiro-Soriano, D. E., & Covin, J. G. (2020). Exploring the viability of equity crowdfunding as a fundraising instrument: A configurational analysis of contingency factors that lead to crowdfunding success and failure. *Journal of Business Research, 115*, 348–356.

DiMaggio, P. J., & Powell, W. W. (1983). The iron cage revisited: Institutional isomorphism and collective rationality in organizational fields. *American Sociological Review, 48*(2), 147–160.

Elliott, M., (2018). Trial by social media: The rise of litigation crowdfunding, 84 University of Cincinnati Law Review. Available at: https://scholarship.law.uc.edu/uclr/vol84/iss2/8

Eckhardt, J. T., Shane, S., & Delmar, F. (2006). Multistage selection and the financing of new ventures. *Management Science, 52*(2), 220–232.

Fazzari, S. M., Hubbard, R. G., & Petersen, B. C. (1988). Financing constraints and corporate investment. *Brookings Papers on Economic Activity, 1*, 141–206.

Frid, C. J., Wyman, D. M., & Gartner, W. B. (2015). The influence of financial'skin in the game'on new venture creation. *Academy of Entrepreneurship Journal, 21*(2), 1.

Fu, J., & Mishra, M. (2022). Fintech in the time of COVID-19: Technological adoption during crises. *Journal of Financial Intermediation, 50*, 100945. ISSN 1042-9573. https://doi.org/10.1016/j.jfi.2021.100945

Fulghieri, P., Garcıa, D., & Hackbarth, D. (2014). *Asymmetric information and the pecking (dis)order, Kenan-Flagler Business School* (Working Paper).

Heminway, J. M., & Hoffman, S. R., (2010). Proceed at your peril: Crowdfunding and the securities act of 1933. *Tennessee Law Review, 78*, 879.

Hofstede, G. (2011). Dimensionalizing cultures: The hofstede model in context. *Online Readings in Psychology and Culture, 2*(1), 2307–0919.

Hornuf, L., & Schwienbacher, A. (2018). Market mechanisms and funding dynamics in equity crowdfunding. *Journal of Corporate Finance, 50*, 556–574.

Jensen, M. C., & Meckling, W. H. (1976). Theory of the firm: Managerial behavior, agency costs and ownership structure. *Journal of Financial Economics, 3*(4), 305–360. https://doi.org/10.2139/ssrn.94043.SSRN94043

Johan, S., & Zhang, Y. (2020). Quality revealing versus overstating in equity crowdfunding. *Journal of Corporate Finance, 65*, 101741.

Jullien, B., & Sand-Zantman, W. (2020, July). The economics of platforms: A theory guide for competition policy. *SSRN Electronic Journal.*

Kirby, E., & Worner, S. (2014). Crowd-funding: An infant industry growing fast. *IOSCO Research Department*, 1–62.

Kleinert, S., & Volkmann, C. (2019). Equity crowdfunding and the role of investor discussion boards. *Venture Capital, 21*(4), 327–352.

Leland, H. E., & Pyle, D. H. (1977). Informational asymmetries, financial structure, and financial intermediation. *The Journal of Finance, 32*(2), 371–387.

Lee, I., & Shin, Y. J. (2018). Fintech: Ecosystem business models investment decisions and challenges. *Business Horizons, 61*(1), 35–46. https://doi.org/10.1016/j.bushor.2017.09.003

Le, M. T. H. (2021). Examining factors that boost intention and loyalty to use Fintech post-COVID-19 lockdown as a new normal behavior. *Heliyon, 7*(8), e07821. ISSN 2405-8440. https://doi.org/10.1016/j.heliyon.2021.e07821

Li, X., Tang, Y., Yang, N., Ren, R., Zheng, H., & Zhou, H. (2016). The value of information disclosure and lead investor in equity-based crowdfunding: An exploratory empirical study. *Nankai Business Review International, 7*(3).

Löher, J., Schneck, S., & Werner, A. (2018). A research note on entrepreneurs' financial commitment and crowdfunding success. *Venture Capital, 20*(3), 309–322.

Lukkarinen, A., Teich, J. E., Wallenius, H., & Wallenius, J. (2016). Success drivers of online equity crowdfunding campaigns. *Decision Support Systems, 87*, 26–38. https://doi.org/10.1016/j.dss.2016.04.006

Ma, Y., & Liu, D. (2017). Introduction to the special issue on Crowdfunding and FinTech. *Financial Innovation, 3.* https://doi.org/10.1186/s40854-017-0058-9

Meoli, M., & Vismara, S. (2021). Information manipulation in equity crowdfunding markets. *Journal of Corporate Finance, 67*, 101866. https://doi.org/10.1016/j.jcorpfin.2020.101866

Modigliani, F., & Miller, M. (1958). The cost of capital, corporate finance, and the theory of investment. *American Economic Review, 3*(48), 261–297.

Mollick, E. (2014). The dynamics of crowdfunding: An exploratory study. *Journal of Business Venturing, 29*, 1–16. https://doi.org/10.1016/j.jbusvent.2013.06.005

Myers, S. C. (1984). The capital structure puzzle. *Journal of Finance, 39*, 575–592.

Myers, S. C., & Majluf, N. (1984). Corporate financing and investment decisions when firms have information that investors do not have. *Journal of Financial Economics, 13*, 187–221.

Nitani, M., Riding, A., & He, B. (2019). On equity crowdfunding: Investor rationality and success factors. *Venture Capital, 21*(2–3), 243–272.

O'Dair, M., & Owen, R. (2019). Financing new creative enterprise through blockchain technology: Opportunities and policy implications. *Strategic Change, 28*(1), 9–17. https://doi.org/10.1002/jsc.2242

Pollack, J. M., Barr, S., & Hanson, S. (2017). New venture creation as establishing stakeholder relationships: A trust-based perspective. *Journal of Business Venturing Insights, 7*, 15–20. ISSN 2352-6734. https://doi.org/10.1016/j.jbvi.2016.12.003

Ralcheva, A., & Roosenboom, P. (2020). Forecasting success in equity crowdfunding. *Small Business Economics, 55*(1), 39–56.

Scharfstein, D. S., & Stein, J. C. (1990). Herd behavior and investment. *The American Economic Review, 80*, 465–479.

Shafi, K. (2021). Investors' evaluation criteria in equity crowdfunding. *Small Business Economics, 56*(1), 3–37.

Signori, A., & Vismara, S. (2018). Does success bring success? the post-offering lives of equity-crowdfunded firms. *Journal of Corporate Finance, 50*, 575–591.

Singh, R. P. (2020). Overconfidence: A common psychological attribute of entrepreneurs which leads to firm failure. *New England Journal of Entrepreneurship.*

Spence, M. (1973). Job market signaling. *The Quarterly Journal of Economics, 87*(3), 355–374.

Spence, M. (2002). Signaling in retrospect and the informational structure of markets. *American Economic Review, 92*(3), 434–459.

Stiglitz, J. E., & Weiss, A. (1981). Credit rationing in markets with imperfect information. *The American Economic Review, 71*(3), 393–410.

Stiglitz, J. E., & Weiss, A. (1983). Alternative approaches to analyzing markets with asymmetric information: Reply. *The American Economic Review, 73*(1), 246–249.

Surowiecki, J. (2005). *The wisdom of crowds*. Anchor.

Vismara, S. (2016). Equity retention and social network theory in equity crowdfunding. *Small Business Economics, 46*(4), 579–590.

Vismara, S. (2018). Information cascades among investors in equity crowdfunding. *Entrepreneurship Theory and Practice, 42*(3), 467–497.

Vrontis, D., Christofi, M., Battisti, E., & Graziano, E. A. (2021). Intellectual capital, knowledge sharing and equity crowdfunding. *Journal of Intellectual Capital, 22*(1), 95–121.

Vulkan, N., ˚Astebro, T., & Sierra, M. F. (2016). Equity crowdfunding: A new phenomena. *Journal of Business Venturing Insights, 5*, 37–49.

Walthoff-Borm, X., Schwienbacher, A., & Vanacker, T. (2018). Equity crowdfunding: First resort or last resort? *Journal of Business Venturing, 33*(4), 513–533. ISSN 0883-9026. https://doi.org/10.1016/j.jbusvent.2018.04.001

Zhang, J., & Liu, P. (2012). Rational herding in microloan markets. *Management Science, 58*(5), 892–912.

CHAPTER 3

# Definition and Description of the Analytical Process: A Data Mining Approach

**Abstract** This section describes the process adopted to gather, process and analyse the data. It starts from the literature about data mining and Knowledge Discovery in databases and follows by describing thoroughly the scraping, wrangling and pre-processing phases also from an applied perspective. The observation period, i.e., when the data mining process has been conducted, goes from May 2019 to October 2020.

**Keywords** Data mining · Web scraping · Knowledge discovery · Data collection · Investor journey · Public information

This study implements a data mining approach since it provides the opportunity to retrace the investor journey—i.e., investor experience. Indeed, the extant literature built and tested theoretical models mostly on data provided directly by ECF platforms or data providers. In some cases, researchers integrated their dataset via hand collection of specific variables. The main differentiation of our study, which we believe to be a strength, lies indeed in the fact that we analysed only data publicly available on the webpages of ECF platforms. Starting by the creation of an account on each platform investigated, we had access to the whole set of information disclosed online. In this way, it was possible to assume the


F. J. Mazzocchini and C. Lucarelli, *Investors' Preferences in Financing New Ventures*,
https://doi.org/10.1007/978-3-031-30058-5_3

point of view of retail investors looking for an investment in ECF and analyse their decision-making process.

We adopted an innovative data mining process to collect the data through data scraping from a large number of platforms (ten) and within an extended timespan in order to gather a unique dataset. To the best of our knowledge, there are no similar studies in extant literature because we were willing to enlarge both the timespan and the cross-country perspective, adding innovation to the existing literature.

Data is in fact collected directly from the websites of several platforms of different nationality through web scraping processes. The analytical phase of the process, conversely, is conducted adopting statistical models to uncover hidden patterns in the dataset and across the different platforms, following a hybrid approach. In fact, adherent to typical data mining approach, our models are data-driven. Then, we discarded data analysis based on machine learning, but rather investigated empirical evidence based on hypothesis deduced from extant literature on the field.

The analytical procedure consists of four main phases: (i) data scraping, (ii) data wrangling, (iii) data pre-processing and (iv) data analysis.

## 3.1 The Knowledge Discovery in Databases (KDD)

The data mining consists of extracting and analyzing large volumes of data in order to discover meaningful relationships and theoretical knowledge (Malik & Rizvi, 2011). It allows to convert raw and unstructured data to knowledge, after a processing and cleaning phase. Data mining is considered the central stages of the Knowledge Discovery in Databases (KDD) process (Fayyad et al., 1996), which is an interactive and iterative process that requires the intervention of the researcher and might result in having recursive stages.

The KDD process involves the following stages:

1. Identification of the purpose of the KDD process and understanding of the application domain;
2. Selection of information sources and data extraction;
3. Data consolidation;
4. Cleaning of the data;
5. Transformation of the data and dimensionality reduction;

6. Data analysis and model selection;
7. Identification of knowledge patterns;
8. Interpretation and reporting of findings.

It is assumed that the first five stages commonly cover about 50–80% of the entire process (Lohr, 2014).

Before beginning the process, the ultimate target of the knowledge discovery process should be clear and well-defined. Having set the goal, the first step is to acquire an understanding of the application domain and get acquainted with the unstructured data available. It is then necessary to select the information sources that might be of interest for the analysis and design an automated data extraction process. Once the extraction process is complete, the raw data must be consolidated, as it oftentimes might come from different sources of information and different formats. Data consolidation consists of collecting, combining (merging) and storing data in a single usable database—i.e., the data warehouse. At this stage, data appears still raw and not suitable for analysis, and it needs to undergo cleaning and wrangling processes, which are commonly conducted via regular expressions or macros. Before being able to extract knowledge patterns, certain features—i.e., variables—need also to be transformed, manipulated or dropped. At this point, the dataset is ready to be analysed. After having selected the appropriate analytical models and identified the main findings, the last step refers to the interpretation, evaluation and documentation of the results.

## 3.2 Data Scraping

One of the first activities of the process is data retrieval. There exist many ways to extract data from information sources and one of them is the data scraping or web scraping. It consists of an automated algorithm that extracts raw data available on the World Wide Web, simulating the human browsing via the Hypertext Transfer Protocol (HTTP). After a preliminary training phase, it scans the webpage to recognize its structure and extract specific raw data via trained selectors.

Briefly, the scraping procedure involves four sub-phases: (i) creation of a sitemap, which represents a file that contains information about the pages and URLs and tells the scraper how to conduct the search, (ii) design of the selector tree (Fig. 3.1) and configuration of the selectors, (iii) training of the scraper, (iv) running the automated algorithm.

**Fig. 3.1** Example of a selector tree

After creating a sitemap, the user identifies the relevant data to pick across the different webpages and their linkages and sets up the algorithm accordingly. The trained selectors will then be able to recognize specific patterns in the webpages' structure and collect the required information automatedly.

In our study, a web scraping algorithm was applied to platforms' websites to extract a set of publicly available information displayed on campaigns' webpages. The procedure was conducted via Webscraper.io that is a Latvian browser extension tool. The automated scraping procedure on a regular monthly basis assured that full data about the whole set of campaigns is originally collected, as some platforms take information off their website as soon as the campaign closes. Similarly, other platforms do not retain on their webpages any record about unsuccessful ventures (e.g., Crowdcube). Indeed, the impermanence and temporariness of information about the campaign and investment outcomes is a characteristic of certain ECF platforms (Butticé & Vismara, 2022). Not only information can be removed by the platform managers, but it might also be modified or altered by entrepreneurs themselves while the financing round is still open. This phenomenon, known as '*information volatility*', represents a considerable barrier to research aiming at retracing the retail investors' decision-making path. However, the implementation of a regular scraping automation circumvents the problem and allows the consolidation of a large comprehensive longitudinal dataset.

Figure 3.2 shows an application of the Webscraper algorithm to extract data via a text selector.

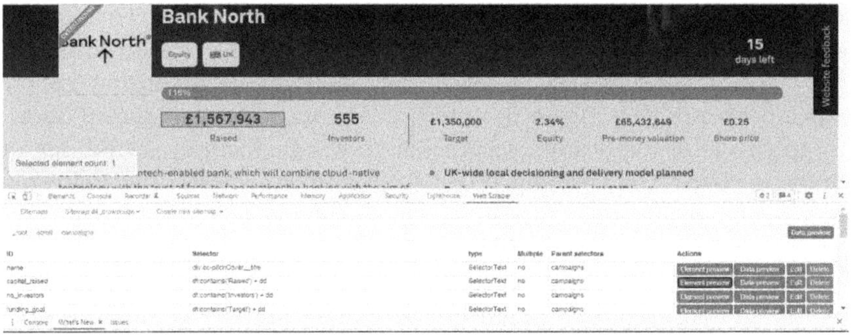


**Fig. 3.2** Example of an application of the webscraper algorithm

## 3.3 Data Consolidation and Wrangling

Information retrieved from webpages consists of raw data that need to be transformed and processed in order to be deposited in a usable dataset (Endel & Piringer, 2015). The whole process is divided into two phases, namely data wrangling and data pre-processing (Kandel et al., 2011). The data wrangling phase refers to the organization and cleaning of the raw dataset. It consists of four basic steps: (i) discovering and understanding the raw data, (ii) organizing and merging the data, (iii) structuring the unstructured data (iv) cleaning the data.

## 3.4 Data Pre-processing

The data pre-processing phase refers to the set of operations of manipulation and transformation of the wrangled dataset to enhance the performance (Alasadi & Bhaya, 2017). It involves different steps: (i) dealing with missing values, (ii) dealing with outliers and noise, (iii) enriching the dataset with additional data, (iv) transforming the variables, (v) encoding of variables and (vi) reducing the dimensionality of the dataset.

## 3.5 Cleaning Procedures in Practice

In our study, data was scraped from different websites and at different times and thus resulted spread over different files. The first step of the data wrangling phase is the conversion of each file from a plain text tabular format (i.e., Comma-Separated Value-CSV) to a spreadsheet. Then the second step is to merge the data files collected from the same platform and append the ones collected either from other platforms or from different time periods, after having indexed the observations according to the extraction period (i.e., from $t_0$ until $t_n$). At this point it might be necessary to check for duplicates and possibly to handle them by combining or removing rows. The cleaning phase then concerns mostly the following tasks:

- conversion of decimal separator (i.e., the symbol that separates the integer part from the fractional part of a number) as different platforms adopts different conventions ranging from the comma till the dot;
- conversion of the SI prefix K for thousand units, which is an informal abbreviation often used on websites or social media;
- suppression of any characters classified as white space between numerical digits (e.g., spaces, tabs, line breaks and special characters such as CHAR(160), etc.) in order to convert numbers stored as text to number format.

Once the wrangling phase is concluded, data is ready to be preprocessed. The main tasks consist of:

- dealing with missing values. For static information (i.e., time invariant), the missing value was derived from previous/subsequent time periods, recalling the information volatility issue of ECF platforms;
- trimming. In some cases, string variables needed to be trimmed in order to remove useless characters (e.g., entrepreneurs' name, age, firm location, etc.);
- generation of dummy and categorical variables from strings (e.g., firm location, gender, campaign success, COVID period, platform, country, etc.);
- generation of numerical variables (e.g., entrepreneur age is calculated in years subtracting the birthdate from the date of fundraising and rounded to the closest integer number; similarly, entrepreneur experience is calculated in years subtracting the designation date from the date of fundraising and rounded to the closest integer number);

- generation and integration of variables via external API tools (e.g., gender dummy variable is obtained via a tool that takes as input the name, surname and nationality of the individual and estimates the gender within a confidence interval);
- generation of complementary variables (e.g., equity retention is obtained subtracting the percentage of shares offered to investors from 100%);
- variables conversion, encoding and destringing;
- currency conversion. Variables expressed in monetary value are converted in Euro at the exchange rate to date of data extraction;
- variables normalization;
- dimensionality reduction;
- drop of observations about unfinished campaigns, keeping only concluded ones;
- data transformation and smoothing (i.e., natural logarithmic transformation, square transformation). Natural logarithmic transformations are applied as: $ln(1 + x)$, as the data contains zeroes;
- enriching the dataset with additional data (i.e., data integration). To prevent the loss of observations, some missing data has been integrated via the scraping of web pages other than the ECF platforms such as the UK governmental Companies House, the social media profiles of the new ventures and entrepreneurs directly accessible through an URL link from the campaign webpage and other ECF data sources (NextFin, Findcrowdfunding, Crunchbase). In some cases, the hand-collection of missing data (Hornuf & Schwienbacher, 2018) was necessary whenever the Webscraper algorithm was not able to effectively retrieve the data.

The final result is an augmented cross-sectional dataset ready for analysis.

## 3.6 Data Analysis

After having retrieved, wrangled, pre-processed and transformed the data, the final steps are data analysis and interpretation/evaluation of the results.

Recalling that analytical models are data-driven, their specification varies across platforms and for dependent variables according to the features extracted. Of those features, part of information was not used for different reasons: it was either heterogeneous across the campaigns (e.g., not present for each campaign), missing or not directly processible. As a consequence, one of the crucial results of our study is that both inter-platform and intra-platform information heterogeneities have to be considered proofs of the absence of institutional isomorphism among ECF platforms.

Data analysis is based on linear and logistic multivariate regressions, which are a type of supervised learning algorithms, to identify knowledge patterns. The models aim at understanding the relationships between dependent and independent variables—i.e., finding the best linear fit, as it is going to be reported in the following chapters.

## References


Alasadi, S. A., & Bhaya, W. S. (2017). Review of data preprocessing techniques in data mining. *Journal of Engineering and Applied Sciences, 12*(16), 4102–4107.

Butticè, V., & Vismara, S. (2022). Inclusive digital finance: The industry of equity crowdfunding. *The Journal of Technology Transfer, 47*, 1224–1241. https://doi.org/10.1007/s10961-021-09875-0

Endel, F., & Piringer, H. (2015). Data wrangling: Making data useful again. *IFACPapersOnLine, 48*(1), 111–112.

Fayyad, U., Piatetsky-Shapiro, G., & Smyth, P. (1996). From data mining to knowledge discovery in databases. *AI Magazine, 17*(3), 37–37.

Hornuf, L., & Schwienbacher, A. (2018). Market mechanisms and funding dynamics in equity crowdfunding. *Journal of Corporate Finance, 50*, 556–574.

Kandel, S., Heer, J., Plaisant, C., Kennedy, J., Van Ham, F., Riche, N. H., Weaver, C., Lee, B., Brodbeck, D., & Buono, P. (2011). Research directions in data wrangling: Visualizations and transformations for usable and credible data. *Information Visualization, 10*(4), 271–288.

Lohr, S. (2014). For data scientists, 'Janitor Work' is hurdle to insights. *The New York Times*, Section B, p. 4.

Malik, S. K., & Rizvi, S. (2011). Information extraction using web usage mining, web scrapping and semantic annotation. *International Conference on Computational Intelligence and Communication Networks, Gwalior, India*, 465–469. https://doi.org/10.1109/CICN.2011.97

CHAPTER 4

# Sample Selection and Platform Characteristics

**Abstract** This section describes the final samples obtained from the data collection phase. It also includes a description of the ECF platforms selected for the investigation (in alphabetic order, 200Crowd, Companisto, Crowdcube, Crowdfunder.com, Fundedbyme, Invesdor, Mamacrowd, Opstart, Seedrs and Sowefund) and of both the target and explanatory variables.

**Keywords** Data collection · Equity crowdfunding · Platforms · Information dissemination · Variables · Scraping

Data is collected directly from the websites of ten ECF platforms of different nationality through regular and automated scraping processes in the period that goes from May 2019 until October 2020. The platforms were chosen for the number of campaigns launched in order to seize cross-cultural effects and increase the dimensionality of the sample. Moreover, the use of multi-platform studies reduces the risk of selection bias (Dushnitsky & Fitza, 2018) and increases the generalizability of our results, when admissible. The data retrieval process was run on a monthly basis and ultimately produced a cross-section dataset of concluded campaigns until October 2020.



F. J. Mazzocchini and C. Lucarelli, *Investors' Preferences in Financing New Ventures*,
https://doi.org/10.1007/978-3-031-30058-5_4

## 4.1 Platform Description

The ten platforms[1] investigated in this study are: *200Crowd, Companisto, Crowdcube, Crowdfunder.com, FundedByMe, Invesdor, Mamacrowd, Opstart, Seedrs and Sowefund*. Here we offer a short description of them, always following an alphabetical order.

*200Crowd* (*Two Hundred crowd*) is an Italian-based ECF platform located in Brescia and currently owned by the 'The Ing Project Srl'. It was founded in 2017 after a successful ECF round of 300,000€ raised on the Tip Ventures portal (former owner and brand name of the portal, active since 2015). It is recognized and authorized by the Italian Companies and Exchange Commission (CONSOB) and operates following the 'all-or-nothing' scheme, with an extended time period provided in case of overfunding. The new brand name, according to Matteo Masserdotti (CEO and Founder of *200Crowd*), derives from the IT, where the 'HTTP 200 OK' success status response code indicates that the server request has succeeded. It is the first Italian ECF platform that uses the syndication investment model, in which investors acquire convertible shares of special purpose vehicles (SPV; i.e., Business angels or venture capitalists) instead of shares of the new venture. The first syndicate ECF campaign was launched in June 2018 for the startup 'Checkout technologies' promoted by Pariter Partners (a group of Business Angels). Until now it has raised over 20 million € from more than 60 campaigns. Its community has more than 20,000 investors.

*Companisto GmbH* is a German-based ECF platform located in Berlin. It was founded in 2012 by the lawyers David Rhotert and Tamo Zwinge and follows a traditional 'all-or-nothing' ECF investment scheme in which investors become shareholders and are entitled to a share of any profits, as well as potentially benefiting from an exit, only in the case in which the minimum funding amount is reached. It is authorized by the German Trade, Commerce and Industry Regulation Act (Gewerbeordnung) and supervised by the BA Friedrichshain-Kreuzberg von Berlin Ordnungs-

[1] Information about the ECF platforms is based on examination of the following websites and their relative social media (as of the end of January 2023): www.200crowd.com, www.companisto.com, www.crowdcube.com, www.crowdfunder.com, www.fundedbyme.com, www.invesdor.com, www.mamacrowd.com, www.opstart.it, www.seedrs.com and www.sowefund.com.

und Gewerbeamt authority. It is currently the largest equity-investment network for startups and SMEs in Germany as it allowed 255 successful financing rounds for an amount of €174 million. Its community has more than 130,000 investors from 92 countries.

*Crowdcube* is located in Exeter, UK and is the largest British ECF platform with over £1.2 billion successfully raised from more than 1,000 campaigns and with a crowd of 1.2 million backers. It was founded in 2011 by Darren Westlake and Luke Lang. The platform works in a traditional 'all-or-nothing' ECF-investment scheme and offers a marketplace not only for equity shares, but also for mini-bonds since 2014. It charges a 7% fee of the amount raised to the founders and in 2018 introduced a 1.5% investor fee (capped at £250) in case of successful collection of the capital. The platform provides consulting services to new ventures in developing business pitches, financial forecasts and principal agency between investors and company. Due to the high number of campaigns published frequently, the platform takes information about unsuccessful campaigns away from the website and here lies the advantage of adopting a data scraping approach. Moreover, the platform provides access to the *Companies House*'s website, which is the UK company register, where ventures provide specific details about their business as required by legislation. *Crowdcube* is authorized to operate in UK by the Financial Conduct Authority since 2013 and is regulated by the Financial Services Authority.

*Crowdfunder.com* was a US-based ECF platform located in Los Angeles. It was founded in 2012 and appears currently not active since September 2020. The platform offered a marketplace for both 'Keep-it-all' ECF-based investments schemes and for syndication investments with a VC owned by the platform (VC Index Fund). The 'keep-it-all' scheme allows the new ventures to keep all the capital raised at the end of a campaign regardless of whether or not the minimum funding goal is reached. The platform allowed for accredited investors only and asked a monthly fee based on different subscription packages (Starter, Premium, Premium Plus) for the use of its platform to both investors and entrepreneurs. However, apart from the subscription fee to list the campaign, *Crowdfunder.com* did not charge any additional fee on the amount raised. Due diligence on new ventures was not performed by the platform, but it was investors' responsibility. Data was retrieved until July 2020, and apparently the platform shut down a few months later.

*Fundedbyme* is a Swedish platform based in Stockholm and operating in Finland, Poland, Malaysia, the Netherlands, Singapore and the United Arab Emirates via joint ventures. It was founded by Arno Smit and Daniel Daboczy in 2011 as a CF-based platform before switching to ECF in 2012, following an 'All-or-nothing' scheme. The platform applies a 1.9% fee on capital invested. *Fundedbyme* got listed at the NGM Nordic MTF stock market in 2019. In late 2021 it merged with another platform, *Pepins*. They changed their name to '*Pepins Group*' and operate with a licence as a securities company under the supervision of the Swedish Financial Supervisory Authority. As of January 2023, *FundedByMe* had raised about €74 million from a crowd of 250,000 backers.

*Invesdor* is located in Helsinki, Finland, and is the first ECF-based platform operating in northern Europe. It was founded in 2012 by Lasse Mäkelä (CEO), Miikka Poutiainen, Petteri Poutiainen, Timo Lappi, Jouni Leskinen and Lare Lekman and in 2015 became the first European ECF platform to obtain MiFID II licence by financial authorities to expand debt and ECF services across all 31 EU and EEA countries. In 2019 Invesdor merged with Nordic and Finnest to form the Invesdor Group Ltd. The platform operates through an 'all-or-nothing' model and is supervised by the Finnish Financial Supervisory Authority. As of January 2023, it has collected about €320 million from 515 campaigns. Its community has more than 124,000 investors.

*Mamacrowd* is the leading Italian ECF-based platform and is located in Milan. It was founded in 2011 by *SiamoSoci Srl* and is currently managed by the same company. It is recognized and authorized by the Italian Companies and Exchange Commission (CONSOB) since 2014. The platform does not charge any fee for the use of the portal and operates following the 'all-or-nothing' model. Since 2020 it offers also a marketplace for real estate crowdfunding campaigns. In 2022 the asset management operator Azimut acquired the majority stake in Mamacrowd. As of January 2023, the platform raised over €182 million from 193 campaigns. Its community has more than 130,000 investors.

*Opstart Srl* is an Italian ECF platform located in Bergamo and founded in 2015. It is recognized and authorized by the Italian Companies and Exchange Commission (CONSOB) and operates following an 'all-or-nothing' scheme. In 2020, during the COVID-19 pandemic, Opstart qualified as the first Italian ECF platform in raising capital. It now recognizes itself as the first Italian FinTech hub as it offers a marketplace for a broad set of fundraising instruments. In fact, it owns nine portals operating with different models: *Opstart* (equity crowdfunding), *Crowdlender* (Peer-to-peer lending), *Crowdbond* (Minibond and debt crowdfunding), *Crowdlisting* (replicates an IPO through the union of equity crowdfunding and direct listing), *Crowdre* (Real Estate crowdfunding), *Crowdbridge* (Bridge financing), *Crowdlegal* (litigation crowdfunding for ventures), *Crowdarena* (first digital bulletin board for the exchange of shares, which resembles a secondary market) and *Tokenbase* (Initial Coin Offerings, Security Token Offerings, Cryptoassets and Blockchain).

*Seedrs* is a British ECF platform located in London and operating also in Lisbon, Portugal. It was originally conceived by Jeff Lynn and Carlos Silva in 2009 as a reward-based CF platform. In 2012 it switched to the ECF model and obtained the authorization to operate in UK by the Financial Conduct Authority, following an 'all-or-nothing' scheme. In June 2017 *Seedrs* became the first ECF platform to launch a (beta) secondary market for allowing crowd-investors to trade ECF stocks of private (unlisted) companies, regardless of whether the companies have run a fundraising campaign on the platform before. *Seedrs* is the second largest platform in the UK, with a funded equity volume of £2.3 billion from 1,876 campaigns as of January 2023. In Q1 2021, a merger deal between *Seedrs* and *Crowdcube* failed due to competition concerns raised by the FCA. The platform was then acquired by the US FinTech platform '*Republic*' in December 2021, and it is its subsidiary since 2022.

*Sowefund* is a French ECF platform located in Paris. It was founded in 2014 by a team of innovation financing and capital investment professionals and is regulated by the Autorité des Marchés Financiers (AMF—i.e., French public authority that regulates financial markets) as a recognized Conseiller en Investissements Participatifs (CIP—i.e., investment advisor). The platform charges between 6 and 10% of the total amount of the fundraising to the new ventures and 1.5% fee to investors for each payment. As of January 2023, Sowefund raised over €68 million from 74 ventures. Its community has about 100,000 investors.

## 4.2 Variables Description

The final augmented dataset is composed of 2,177 ventures observed at a monthly frequency, for a total of thirteen time periods, from the 10 ECF platforms.

Due to its low frequency of scraping and due to the average length of a campaign, generally between thirty and sixty days, this dataset analyzes data of concluded campaigns without time-varying effects. Moreover, the dataset also includes information about campaigns concluded before the scraping period, whenever publicly available on the platforms' website. Hence, it is a 'static' cross-sectional dataset, as observation about unconcluded campaigns (or preceding time periods) has been ruled out.

Recalling that some of the variables used in the empirical settings are not commonly available for all the platforms, there persist instances of missing values for certain observations. Therefore, not all the models were able to use all the variables (as for Nitani et al., 2019) and presented different specifications, due to the nature of information dissemination. In addition to that, although available, in certain models variables had to be dropped due to multicollinearity issues (i.e., pairwise correlations above 0.8 and Variance Inflation Factor tests above 10; Belinda & Peat, 2014; Shrestha, 2020; Young, 2017).

Note that in certain model specifications, monetary variables are subject to logarithmic transformations (labelled with the symbol '§'), after currency conversion. This improves the fit of the models by reducing distributions' skewness. Moreover, in some specification we investigate the presence of a quadratic relationship as well (labelled with the symbol '^').

### *4.2.1 Dependent Variables*

In this empirical analysis, the success of an individual crowdfunding campaign is measured as the ability to raise the targeted amount of capital within the campaign. In this regard, success is driven by the preferences of investors (i.e., willingness-to-invest). Therefore, we identified five proxies for success: campaign success (Y1), percentage of funding raised (Y2), amount of capital raised (Y3), number of investors (Y4), presence of professional investors (Y5).

(Y1) *Campaign success*: is a dichotomous variable that measures whether the pre-determined minimum funding target has been reached (=1) or not (=0) within the fundraising period. In other words, it expresses whether the amount raised equals or exceeds the amount targeted. The variable is generated through regular expressions and took the value of 1 if the web scraper detected the label 'financed' (e.g., 'Financed', 'Financé', 'Finanziata', etc.) in the respective HTML section of the campaign's website, and/or if the ratio (automatedly calculated on the spreadsheets) between capital raised and minimum funding goal is equal or exceeding 1. The variable took the value of 0 otherwise, i.e., the campaign is labelled as 'not financed' and/or the ratio is lower than 1, subject to the condition that data is not missing.

(Y2) *Percentage of funding raised*: measures the percentage of capital raised as the ratio between the total amount of capital raised and the minimum financing goal, recalling that the new venture will be financed on the condition that at least 100% of percentage of funding is reached, and captures the financial engagement of investors (both retail and professional).

(Y3) *Amount of capital raised*: measures the total amount of capital raised (in monetary value) during the campaign.

(Y4) *Number of investors*: measures the number of crowd-investors that have supported the campaign, thus capturing the wisdom-of-the-crowd. Beyond the number, the variable most importantly reflects the success of a campaign in that it bridges the gap between capital required and capital effectively raised.

(Y5) *Presence of professional investors*: is a dummy variable that signals whether a professional investor (e.g., financial intermediaries, venture capitalists, business angels, etc.) has bid and secured shares in the new ventures.

### *4.2.2 Independent Variables*

As already stated, drivers for crowd-investors' preferences are identified across four categories: human, financial and social capital of entrepreneurs (K1), venture characteristics (K2), campaign characteristics (K3) and investors' behaviour (K4). Each category is proxied by a set of explanatory variables that represents information and signals publicly available on the platform websites.

The first category (K1) contains: entrepreneur experience, entrepreneur age, entrepreneur gender, equity retention, social media presence, social media count.

- *Entrepreneur age*: is a numerical generated variable that reflects the age of the entrepreneur in years (at the time of fundraising);
- *Entrepreneur gender*: is a dummy-generated variable reflecting the gender of the primary owner (=1) if female (=0) if male. The variable is generated via a tool (Genderize.io) that estimates the gender from the name, surname and nationality of an individual within a certain confidence interval. Not-significant estimates were then revised by the author and hand-collected;
- *Entrepreneur experience*: is a numerical generated variable that represents the number of years in which the current owner has been performing the role of director within the same firm (i.e., seniority);
- *Equity retention*: measures the percentage of the firm's share retained by the entrepreneur(s). It reflects not only their financial commitment, but also their skin-in-the-game and their risk appetite (Cassar, 2004), which in some cases might also verge on overconfidence. It is generated as the complement to 100 of the percentage of shares offered, which represent the percentage of firms' shares offered to future shareholders (in case of successful ECF campaign). Shares offered is a publicly available piece of information that can be retrieved from the campaign website;
- *Social media presence*: captures the presence of the entrepreneur(s) on social media either with their own account or with their venture's. The variable is generated as a dummy and takes on the value of 1 whether the new venture provided information (e.g., active URLs) to its social media accounts—i.e., at least one between LinkedIn, Twitter, Facebook and Instagram—or not (=0) subject to the condition that the ECF platform provided a common HTML section on its website for this information;
- *Social media count*: reflects the usage of social media networks to promote the ECF campaign and the business idea by counting the number of direct links to social media web pages. It measures the quantity of social/alliance capital accessible from the campaign's page (Facebook, Twitter, Instagram, LinkedIn).

The second category (K2) contains: financial forecast, financial forecast (year), equity, pre-money valuation, outstanding shares, firm location, firm maturity.

- *Financial forecast*: it is a financial metric that measures the predicted revenues that the venture would generate in the next years with the funding raised from a successful campaign;
- *Financial forecast (year)* : indicates the year in which the predicted revenues would be achieved;
- *Equity*: it is a financial metric that measures the net balance of the firm's assets reduced by the liabilities;
- *Pre-money valuation*: it is a financial metric that measures the estimated value (in Euro) of the venture before launching the ECF campaign, as evaluated by analysts/advisors and/or consultants;
- *Outstanding shares*: it is a financial metric that indicates the number of ECF stocks issued, taking into account the stock split and conversion;
- *Firm location*: measures whether the new venture's registered office is located in the same country of the ECF platform in which it is listed. It reflects the geographical and cultural proximity. It is a dummy variable generated by matching the locations of the two parties that takes the value of 1 in case of positive matching and 0 otherwise;
- *Firm maturity*: is a numerical generated variable that measures the age of the firm in years since its establishment.

The third category (K3) contains: share price, minimum funding target, maximum funding target, maximum retail investment, COVID period.

- *Share price*: measures the price for a single ECF share of the firm; in other words, it represents the minimum investment required to a single investor for a bid to be eligible;
- *Minimum funding goal*: the minimum (floor) target amount of capital (in Euro) to be raised to reach the funding goal (i.e., campaign success);
- *Maximum funding goal*: is the maximum (cap) amount of capital (in Euro) that could be raised. It is set by the entrepreneurs to allow for overfunding and at the same time avoid excessive dilution of the control shares;

- *Maximum retail investment*: measures the maximum amount of capital that can be subscribed from retail investors (in Euro); the remaining part is reserved for professionals;
- *COVID period*: it is a dummy-generated variable that states whether the fundraising campaign was launched during the COVID-19 pandemic (=1; from March 2020) or earlier (=0).

The fourth category (K4) contains: interested investors, percentage raised, amount of capital raised, number of investors, presence of professional investors.

- *Interested investors*: measures the number of potential investors that expressed interest in the campaign (through a click on the campaign's website) and follow its updates;
- *Percentage raised*: identical meaning to the dependent Y2, but here used as explanatory variable;
- *Amount of capital raised*: identical meaning to the dependent Y3, but here used as explanatory variable;
- *Number of investors*: identical meaning to the dependent Y4, but here used as explanatory variable;
- *Presence of professional investors*: identical meaning to the dependent Y5, but here used as explanatory variable.

In addition to dependent and explanatory variables, other variables are created in order to partition the database in subsets but are not used for estimates. Among all:

- *Platform dummy*: categorical-generated variable that controls for the platform on which the venture is listed;
- *Country dummy*: categorical-generated variable that controls for the platform country on which the venture is listed.

## 4.3 Information Dissemination

In this section, we described the main information extracted from the platform websites that served as dependent or independent variables in our models. We recall that model specifications vary across platforms/countries and also for type of dependent variable. However, this might depend not only on the absence of information, but also on model specification and multicollinearity issues. In particular, the former case comprehends cases in which either the information is not provided by the platform, or the information was not homogeneously displayed in its website, which means that the scraping algorithm was not able to identify a clear HTML layout.

Moreover, the data scraping process was able to extract also additional pieces of publicly available information that were not suitable for the analytical models. Whenever possible, this information was converted into a variable (e.g., creation of categorical or dummy variables from strings of text extracted). In the other cases, data remained unstructured and for this reason does not appear in our analyses.

Therefore, information dissemination from ECF platforms might be wider than the one reported in these models.

### *4.3.1 Data Available Per Platform*

This subsection provides an overview of the variables (i.e., pieces of information) available for each of the platforms investigated in the study among the ones that were suitable for the analysis. The following table (see Table 4.1) summarizes it as follows. For each platform, indicated as columns, variables are ordered starting with the dependent variables to the explanatory variables. The latter are listed following the category order (i.e., from K1 to K4). Dark-coloured cells indicate the presence of the variable, scraped or generated, whereas blank cells indicate their absence.

**Table 4.1** Variables available in the dataset

| | ECF platform / Variable name | 200Crowd | companisto | crowdcube | crowdfunder | fundedbyme | invesdor | mamacrowd | opstart | seedrs | sowefund |
|---|---|---|---|---|---|---|---|---|---|---|---|
| **Success dimensions** | campaign success | | | | | | | | | | |
| | percentage of funding raised | | | | | | | | | | |
| | amount of capital raised | | | | | | | | | | |
| | number of investors | | | | | | | | | | |
| | presence of professional investors | | | | | | | | | | |
| **K1: Entrepreneur human financial and social capital** | entrepreneur age | | | | | | | | | | |
| | entrepreneur gender | | | | | | | | | | |
| | entrepreneur experience | | | | | | | | | | |
| | equity retention | | | | | | | | | | |
| | social media presence | | | | | | | | | | |
| | social media count | | | | | | | | | | |
| **K2: Venture characteristics** | financial forecast | | | | | | | | | | |
| | financial forecast (year) | | | | | | | | | | |
| | equity | | | | | | | | | | |
| | pre-money valuation | | | | | | | | | | |
| | outstanding shares | | | | | | | | | | |
| | firm location | | | | | | | | | | |
| | firm maturity | | | | | | | | | | |
| **K3: Campaign characteristics** | share price | | | | | | | | | | |
| | minimum funding target | | | | | | | | | | |
| | maximum funding target | | | | | | | | | | |
| | maximum retail investment | | | | | | | | | | |
| | COVID period | | | | | | | | | | |
| **K4: Investors behaviours** | interested investors | | | | | | | | | | |
| | percentage raised | | | | | | | | | | |
| | amount of capital raised | | | | | | | | | | |
| | number of investors | | | | | | | | | | |
| | presence of professional investors | | | | | | | | | | |

## References


Belinda, B., & Peat, J. (2014). *Medical statistics: A guide to SPSS, data analysis, and critical appraisal* (2nd ed.). Wiley.

Cassar, G., (2004). The financing of business start-ups. *Journal of Business Venturing*, *19*(2), 261–283.

Dushnitsky, G., & Fitza, M. A. (2018). Are we missing the platforms for the crowd? Comparing investment drivers across multiple crowdfunding platforms. *Journal of Business Venturing Insights, 10*, e00100.

Nitani, M., Riding, A., & He, B. (2019). On equity crowdfunding: Investor rationality and success factors. *Venture Capital, 21*(2–3), 243–272.

Shrestha, N. (2020). Detecting multicollinearity in regression analysis. *American Journal of Applied Mathematics and Statistics, 8*, 39–42. https://doi.org/10.12691/ajams-8-2-1

Young, D. S. (2017). *Handbook of regression methods* (pp. 109–136). CRC Press.

CHAPTER 5

# Data Analysis and Econometric Models

**Abstract** This section provides an overview of the data analysis performed and of the econometric models adopted to test the research hypotheses. It begins by introducing the strategy of analysis, follows with a review of the main findings obtained from extant literature, which represents the benchmark for our comparison, and concludes by explaining the analytical models adopted to test the research hypotheses.

**Keywords** Data analysis · Regression · Econometric models · Success · Entrepreneurs · Human capital · Social capital · Venture · Investors' behaviour

As anticipated in Chapter 1, one of the innovations of this research is the *hybrid* data analysis approach. In fact, we merge innovative tools of data mining, to grab all the public information available in platform websites, with traditional methods of testing hypothesis expected from extant literature. Contrarily to the pattern of knowledge discovery that should complement the data mining process with a machine learning process, here we exploit the data collected to verify confirmation or innovation of knowledge accumulated by established conventional research.



F. J. Mazzocchini and C. Lucarelli, *Investors' Preferences in Financing New Ventures*,
https://doi.org/10.1007/978-3-031-30058-5_5

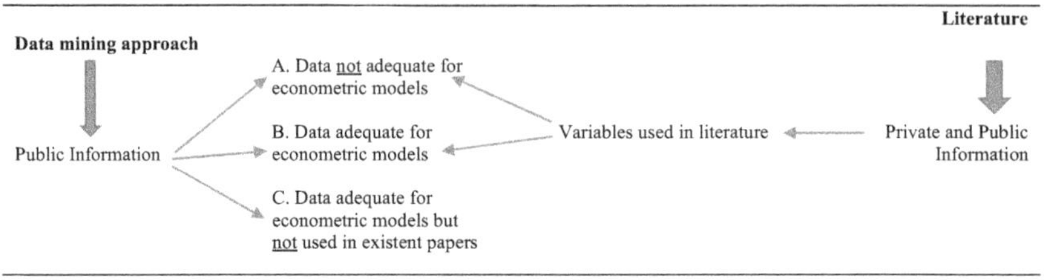


**Fig. 5.1** Organization of data to run econometric models vis-a-vis existent literature

The reconciliation underlying this *hybrid* approach needs to categorise the typologies of information collected. The data mining, as described in Chapter 3, allowed us to collect three kinds of data: first, information retrieved from web-sites than can be recalled to variables already studied by existent literature to unfold dynamics of financing new ventures via ECF, but that are too occasional, or limited within the various campaigns of a given platform, or also too rare in the inter-platform comparison (from Fig. 5.1, Data typology A). Moreover, we collected data recallable to variables already used in existent literature, that hold width and frequency adequate to be employed in econometric models (from Fig. 5.1, Data typology B). Finally, the approach of data mining itself, based on regular storing of data on monthly basis for a year for a sample of platform websites, allowed us to obtain new information, not already present in existing literature (from Fig. 5.1, Data typology C). Everything considered, we anticipate here that, at the end of this Chapter, we show how we reconcile the 12 research hypotheses that we designed in Chapter 2 (Table 2.2) with the evidence of specific findings that are quite scattered, in ECF literature.

As already stated, our dependent variable is related to the idea of the ECF success and connected to investors' preferences in financing new ventures. This idea can be objectivized and measured by different indicators, that in turn may represent different alternative dependent variables for our econometric models: the campaign success (Y1); the percentage of capital raised[1] (Y2); the monetary value of capital raised (Y3); the number of investors (Y4); the presence of professional investors (Y5). Note that, in the literature, only four of our five typologies of dependent variable

[1] We recall that the information of percentage of capital raised is explicitly given by some platforms (e.g., the Italian Mamacrowd); for other platform this figure has been obtained by authors as the ratio of capital raised on the funding goal.

**Table 5.1** Drivers of investors' behaviour and groups of independent variables

| *K1: Entrepreneur human financial and social capital (6)* | *K2: Venture characteristics (7)* | *K3: Campaign characteristics (5)* | *K4: Investors behaviours (5)* |
|---|---|---|---|
| Entrepreneur age | Financial forecast (year) | Share price | Interested investors |
| Entrepreneur gender | Financial forecast | Min. funding target | Percentage raised |
| Entrepreneur experience | Equity | Max. funding target | Capital raised |
| Equity retention | Pre-money | Max. retail investment | Number of investors |
| Social media presence | Outstanding shares | COVID period | Professional investors |
| Social media count | Firm location | | |
| | Firm maturity | | |

*Note* In the first raw in bracket, we indicate the (maximum) number of variables for each group

have been explored, as to our knowledge the Y5 variable, indicating presence of professional investors, has not been directly studied yet for the platforms that provide publicly this piece of information. This represents an example of exploitation of data belonging to typology C of Fig. 5.1.

Regarding the independent variables, as shown in Fig. 2.1, from the existing literature we selected four main drivers that might influence investors' behaviour, and definitively affect the success of the campaign. As described in Chapter 2, these drivers are related to: (1) entrepreneur's human, financial and social capital; (2) venture characteristics; (3) campaign characteristics and (4) investors' behaviour itself. Coherently, we grouped these independent variables, present in existing literature, in corresponding four groups (from K1 to K4). The data mind procedure, addressed to store any available structured information from the main ECF platforms, induced us to select a list of variables, belonging to each of these clusters, and able to represent a dimension that could drive investors' choice, as shown by Table 5.1.

Remember that the selection of these variables is definitively data-driven, resulting from the procedure that collected the public information which we valued adequate to be included in econometric models (Data typology B and C of Fig. 5.1).

To be precise, part of the extracted and stored data appears valid to individuate/compute independent variables for econometric modelling, but they seem to be not considered by literature. They clearly belong to Data typology C and are these seven variables: Financial forecast (amount), Financial forecast (year), Equity, Outstanding shares, Max. funding target, Max. retail investment and Interested investors. The COVID period variable has been created by authors as they extracted data on monthly basis for a year, including the event of the pandemic. So, they controlled for this event including a 'time' dummy variable (COVID period is 0 for campaigns concluded before March 2020; 1 otherwise).

## 5.1 Review of the Main Findings from Literature

From now on, we focus on Data typology B and in the following we show how the existing literature already used these variables to investigate their relationship with the ECF success. Specifically, various studies already considered the effect of (some) of our independent variables on specific measures for our dependent variables. This implicates that we could have, from the literature, an indication of the expect sign of these connections. Nevertheless, in the following, we report existing evidence, with specific indication of both the dependent variable considered and the platform (s) explored (see Tables from L3 to L6). Note that in this chapter the list of platforms observed is ordered following a mere alphabetic rule. In the next Chapter 6, we reorder platforms following a country-specific rule.

We anticipate that results are often contradictory, given the various combination of platform/measure of success. Moreover, we need to point out that the literature existent in our knowledge, up to now, neglected the study of campaign's success for two platforms: 200Crowd and Opstart. Consequently, for these two platforms data collected results as Data typology C.

Firstly, we consider the Y1 variable, which stands for the campaign success measured as a binary variable indicating 1, if the target goal has been reached, and 0 elsewhere. Given this specific dependent variable, we have a list of studies frequently showing concordant findings, but sometimes offering inconsistent evidence. Table 5.2 offers summary of the relationships proven by existing literature, with a visual/colour support to indicate if the link has been found significantly positive or negative, according to the following association, that is going to work also in Tables from 5.3 to 5.5.

| + | "+/0" | 0 | "+/–" | "–/0" | – |
|---|---|---|---|---|---|
| Concordant literature showing significant positive relationship | Not concordant literature showing either significant positive or not significant relationship | Concordant literature showing not significant relationship | Not concordant literature showing significant either positive or negative relationship | Not concordant literature showing either significant negative or not significant relationship | Concordant literature showing significant negative relationship |

The binary variable Y1 is the most studied in existing literature to indicate the success of an ECF campaign, and, as shown by Table 5.2,

**Table 5.2** Relationships between campaign success (Y1) and clusters of independent variables

| | | Companisto | Crowdcube | Crowdfunder | Fundedbyme | Invesdor | Mamacrowd | Seedrs |
|---|---|---|---|---|---|---|---|---|
| Entrepreneur age | K1 | | Ralcheva and Roosenboom, 2020 (-) | | | | | Ralcheva and Roosenboom, 2020 (-) |
| Entrepreneur gender | K1 | | Barbi and Mattioli, 2019 (0); De Crescenzo et al. 2020 (+) | | | | Piva and Rossi-Lamastra, 2018 (0) | |
| Entrepreneur experience | K1 | Nitani et al. 2019 (+) | Cumming et al, 2019 (+); Nitani et al. 2019 (+); Vismara, 2019 (0); Kleinert et al. 2020 (+); Shafi 2021 (0) | Mamonov and Malaga 2019 (0) | Nitani et al. 2019 (+) | Nitani et al. 2019 (+) | Piva and Rossi-Lamastra, 2018 (+) | Cumming et al, 2019 (+); Vismara, 2019 (0) |
| Equity retention | K1 | | Cumming et al, 2019 (+); Vismara, 2019 (+); Ralcheva and Roosenboom, 2020 (+); Shafi 2021 (+) | | | | | Cumming et al, 2019 (+); Vismara, 2019 (+); Ralcheva and Roosenboom, 2020 (+) |
| Social media presence/ count | K1 | Nitani et al. 2019 (+) | Nitani et al. 2019 (+) | | Nitani et al. 2019 (+) | Nitani et al. 2019 (+) | Piva and Rossi-Lamastra, 2018[a] (+) | |
| Financial forecast | K2 | Nitani et al. 2019 (+) | Nitani et al. 2019 (+) | | Nitani et al. 2019 (+) | Nitani et al. 2019 (+) | | |
| Pre-money | K2 | | Coakley et al. 2022 (-) | | | | | Coakley et al. 2022 (-) |
| Firm location | K2 | | Shafi 2021 (0); Coakley et al. 2022 (0) | | | | | Coakley et al. 2022 (0) |
| Firm maturity | K2 | Nitani et al. 2019 (-) | Cumming et al, 2019 (-); Nitani et al. 2019 (-); De Crescenzo et al. 2020 (0); Ralcheva and Roosenboom, 2020 (-); Shafi 2021 (0); Coakley et al. 2022 (+) | Mamonov and Malaga 2019 (+) | Nitani et al. 2019 (-) | Nitani et al. 2019 (-) | | Cumming et al, 2019 (-); Ralcheva and Roosenboom, 2020 (0); Coakley et al. 2022 (+) |
| Min funding target | K3 | | Cumming et al, 2019 (0); Ralcheva and Roosenboom, 2020 (0; but - for both crowdcube and seedrs jointly) | | | | Piva and Rossi-Lamastra, 2018 (-) | Vulkan et al 2016 (-); Cumming et al, 2019 (0); Ralcheva and Roosenboom, 2020 (0; but - for both crowdcube and seedrs jointly) |
| Number of investors | K4 | | Coakley et al. 2022 (+) | | | | | Vulkan et al 2016 (+); Coakley et al. 2022 (+) |
| Professional investors | K4 | | | Mamonov and Malaga 2019 (+) | | | | |

[a]Number of LinkedIn connections

papers that have been investigating this expression of success involving the largest number (seven) of platforms. Variables referring to the characteristics of the entrepreneur (K1 cluster) have been largely studied with, most of the times, concordant evidence. Youth, financial commitment of the entrepreneur and her social capital significantly and positively affect the success of ECF campaigns, for the papers considered, while less converging evidence results for the entrepreneur experience and her gender. Withing the K2 cluster, while for the financial forecast variable there is a steady convergence of literature showing a significant positive relationship with campaign's success, the role of the remaining variables seems to be differently appreciated within the various platform considered. The effect of firm maturity appears as the most ambiguous in existing papers. For cluster K3 we have evidence only for the (disclosure of the) minimum funding target and studies in Mamacrowd and Seedrs agree with a significative negative influence on campaign's success, while in Crowdcube and Seedrs literature is concordant in finding no significant relationship. Finally, the active participation of investors, in terms of both their numerosity and presence of institutional investors, consistently affects positively the success of the campaign.

When changing the indication for the success of an ECF campaign, and consider the capital raised, either in relation to the funding goal (Y2) or in monetary value (Y3), evidence appear scattered (consider Tables 5.3 and 5.4). Aside some convergent evidence for presence in social media and entrepreneurial experience of K1 cluster, pre-money of cluster K2 and number of investors of cluster K4, remaining findings appeared somehow puzzled in contradictory evidence. As an example, the influence of equity retention appears supported with very inconsistent sign; the minimum funding target, if, on the one hand, consistently negatively affects the percentage of capital raised (Y2), on the other hand it positively affects the amount of capital raised (Y3).

Moving to Table 5.5, here we consider a different proxy of ECF success, that has been considered by some part of the literature, and is the number of investors, representing our Y4 dependent variable.

Here, evidence appears less jeopardized even if platforms investigated are various (five) with variables belonging to cluster K1 mostly generally proved to positively influence this dimension of campaign's success, while, interestingly, firm maturity of K2, seems to positively affect the number of investors Y4, coherent with Y3, even if in various papers the influence

**Table 5.3** Relationships between percentage of capital raised (Y2) and clusters of independent variables

| | | Companisto | Crowdfunder | Mamacrowd | Seedrs | Sowefund |
|---|---|---|---|---|---|---|
| Entrepreneur age | K1 | Löher et al 2018 (-) | | | | |
| Entrepreneur gender | K1 | | Dority et al. 2021 (0) | Piva and Rossi-Lamastra, 2018 (0) | | Andrieu et al. 2021 (-) |
| Equity retention | K1 | Löher et al 2018 (+) | | | | |
| Social media presence/count | K1 | | | Piva and Rossi-Lamastra, 2018[1] (+) | | |
| Pre-money | K2 | Löher et al 2018 (+) | | | | |
| Firm location | K2 | | | | | Andrieu et al. 2021 (0) |
| Firm maturity | K2 | | | | | Andrieu et al. 2021 (0) |
| Min funding target | K3 | | Dority et al. 2021 (-) | Piva and Rossi-Lamastra, 2018 (-) | Vulkan et al 2016 (-) | Andrieu et al. 2021 (-) |
| Number of investors | K4 | | | | Vulkan et al 2016 (+) | |
| Professional investors | K4 | Löher et al 2018 (0) | | | | |

**Table 5.4** Relationships between $ capital raised (Y3) and clusters of independent variables

| | | Crowdcube | Crowdfunder | Invesdor | Seedrs |
|---|---|---|---|---|---|
| Entrepreneur gender | K1 | Vismara 2016 (–) | | | Vismara 2016 (–) |
| Entrepreneur experience | K1 | Barbi and Mattioli 2019 (0); Shafi 2021 (+) | Lim and Busenitz 2020 (+) | | |
| Equity retention | K1 | Vismara 2016 (+); Shafi 2021 (+); Coakley et al. 2022 (–) | | | Vismara 2016 (+); Coakley et al. 2022 (–) |
| Social media presence/count | K1 | Vismara 2016 (+); Barbi and Mattioli 2019 (0) | | Lukkarinen et al. 2016 (+) | Vismara 2016 (+) |
| Premoney | K2 | Coakley et al. 2022 (+) | | | Coakley et al. 2022 (+) |
| Firm location | K2 | Shafi 2021 (0); Coakley et al. 2022 (0) | Lim and Busenitz 2020 (0) | | Coakley et al. 2022 (0) |
| Firm maturity | K2 | Barbi and Mattioli 2019 (+); Shafi 2021 (0); Coakley et al. 2022 (+) | | | Coakley et al. 2022 (+) |
| Share price | K3 | | | Lukkarinen et al. 2016 (–) | |
| Min funding target | K3 | Kleinert et al. 2020 (+); Shafi 2021 (+); Coakley et al. 2022 (+) | Lim and Busenitz 2020 (+) | Lukkarinen et al. 2016 : (+) | Coakley et al. 2022 (+) |
| Number of investors | K4 | Kleinert and Volkmann 2019 (+); Coakley et al. 2022 (+) | | | Coakley et al. 2022 (+) |
| Professional investors | K4 | | Lim and Busenitz 2020 (0) | | |

**Table 5.5** Relationships between number of investors (Y4) and clusters of independent variables

| | | Companisto | Crowdcube | Invesdor | Mamacrowd | Seedrs |
|---|---|---|---|---|---|---|
| Entrepreneur gender | K1 | | Barbi and Mattioli 2019 (+) | | Piva and Rossi-Lamastra 2018 (0) | |
| Entrepreneur experience | K1 | | Cumming et al. 2019 (+); Kleinert et al. 2020 (+); Barbi and Mattioli 2019 (0) | | Piva and Rossi-Lamastra 2018 (+) | Cumming et al. 2019 (+); Vismara 2019 (0) |
| Equity retention | K1 | Block et al. 2018 (0) | Vismara 2016 (+); Vismara 2019 (+) | | | Vismara 2016 (+); Vismara 2019 (+) |
| Social media presence/count | K1 | | Vismara 2016 (+); Barbi and Mattioli 2019 (0) | Lukkarinen et al. 2016 (+) | Piva and Rossi-Lamastra 2018 (number of LinkedIn connections +) | Vismara 2016 (+) |
| Firm maturity | K2 | | Barbi and Mattioli 2019 (+) | | | |
| Share price | K3 | | | Lukkarinen et al. 2016 (–) | | |
| Min funding target | K3 | | Vismara 2016 (+); Vismara 2019 (+) | Lukkarinen et al. 2016 : (+) | Piva and Rossi-Lamastra 2018 (0) | Vismara 2016 (+); Vismara 2019 (+) |

appears not-significant for Y2, and with very contradictory evidences for the Y1 dependent variable.

To sum up, Table 5.6 offers the list of the independent variables known by literature, inferable from the public information that we collected through the data mining, and usable in our econometric models (Data typology B). Nevertheless, evidence of findings offered by ECF literature appears quite scattered, indeed. In Tables from 5.2 to 5.5, we show that findings are convergent only in few cases/variables and, most of the time, the relationship of explanatory variables with the campaign success, is mutable, depending on both the ECF platform observed, and metric of success (Y) considered. For this reason, in Table 5.6, in the column addressed to give the evidence offered by existing ECF literature, we reported the expression '*contradictory/platform-specific/Y-specific*'.

Nevertheless, our *hybrid* data analysis approach forces us to test the knowledge accumulated by established conventional research. This imposes us to recall the list of research hypotheses that we designated in Chapter 2 (Table 2.2) and settle them within such a various literature, with explicit acknowledgement that in most cases the expected relationship allows 'alternative expectations'.

## 5.2 Methodology of Estimation

Finally, moving on to the estimation methodology, Table 5.7 indicates the various estimators, mainly induced by the nature of the measure used to indicate the dependent variable.

Note that specific metrics, namely, Y2, Y3, Y4 and Y5, when not used as dependent variable in econometric models, they are going to be included as expression of investors' behaviour, thus belonging to the K4 cluster, as well.

**Table 5.6** Junction among Data typology B—existing ECF literature—research hypotheses

| *K* | *Independent variables Inferable from Data typology B* | *Evidence from existing ECF literature* | *RH* | *Expected relationship* |
|---|---|---|---|---|
| K1 | Entrepreneur age | Consistently negative | H1.a | Negative |
| K1 | Entrepreneur gender | Contradictory/platform-specific/Y-specific | H1.b | Alternative expectations |
| K1 | Entrepreneur experience | Mostly positive | H1.c | Positive |
| K1 | Equity retention | Contradictory/platform-specific/Y-specific | H2 | Alternative expectations |
| K1 | Social media presence/count | Mostly positive | H3 | Positive |
| K2 | Financial forecast | Consistently positive | H4 | Positive |
| K2 | Pre-money | Contradictory/platform-specific/Y-specific | H5 | Alternative expectations |
| K2 | Firm location | Consistently not significant | H6 | Positive[2] |
| K2 | Firm maturity | Mostly positive but platform-specific/Y-specific | H7 | Positive |
| K3 | Share price | Consistently negative (by rare observations) | H8 | Negative |
| K3 | Min funding target | Mainly negative but platform-specific/Y-specific | H9 | Negative |
| K4 | Percentage raised | Studied as dependent variable; not studied as independent variable | H10.a | Positive |
| K4 | Capital raised | Consistently not significant | H10.b | Positive |
| K4 | Number of investors | Consistently positive | H11 | Positive |
| K4 | Professional investors | Mostly positive | H12 | Positive |

[2] Note that here the expected positive link is due to a literature non-specifically referred to ECF (Agrawal et al., 2015), given for this case results appear not-significant.

**Table 5.7** Dependent variables and econometric models

| *Dependent variable* | | *Nature of the variable* | *Estimation* | *Model* |
|---|---|---|---|---|
| Y1 | Campaign success | Binary variable (0–1) | Logit | Mod (1) |
| Y2/K4 | Percentage raised | Continuous (%; in some cases exceeding 100%) | Linear-log regression | Mod (2) |
| Y3/K4 | Capital raised | Monetary value | Linear regression | Mod (3a) |
| | | Log of capital raised | Log-linear regression | Mod (3b) |
| | | Log of capital raised | Log-log regression | Mod (3c) |
| Y4/K4 | Number of investors | Continuous (count) | Linear-log regression | Mod (4) |
| Y5/K4 | Professional investors | Binary variable (0–1) | Logit | Mod (5) |

## References


Agrawal, A., Catalini, C., & Goldfarb, A. (2015). Crowdfunding: Geography, social networks, and the timing of investment decisions. *Journal of Economics & Management Strategy*, *24*(2), 253–274.

Ahlers, G. K., Cumming, D., Günther, C., & Schweizer, D. (2015). Signaling in equity crowdfunding. *Entrepreneurship Theory and Practice, 39*(4), 955–980.

Andrieu, G., Le Pendeven, B., & Leboeuf, G. (2021). Equity crowdfunding success for female entrepreneurs: French evidence. *Economics Bulletin, 41*(2).

Barbi, M., & Mattioli, S. (2019). Human capital, investor trust, and equity crowdfunding. *Research in International Business and Finance, 49*, 1–12.

Coakley, J., Lazos, A., & Liñares-Zegarra, J. M. (2022). Equity crowdfunding founder teams: Campaign success and venture failure. *British Journal of Management, 33*(1), 286–305.

Cumming, D., Meoli, M., & Vismara, S. (2019). Investors' choices between cash and voting rights: Evidence from dual-class equity crowdfunding. *Research Policy, 48*(8), 103740.

De Crescenzo, V., Ribeiro-Soriano, D. E., & Covin, J. G. (2020). Exploring the viability of equity crowdfunding as a fundraising instrument: A configurational analysis of contingency factors that lead to crowdfunding success and failure. *Journal of Business Research, 115*, 348–356.

Dority, B., Borchers, S. J., & Hayes, S. K. (2021). Equity crowdfunding: Us title ii offerings using sentiment analysis. *Studies in Economics and Finance*.

Hornuf, L., & Schwienbacher, A. (2018). Market mechanisms and funding dynamics in equity crowdfunding. *Journal of Corporate Finance, 50*, 556–574.

Kleinert, S., & Volkmann, C. (2019). Equity crowdfunding and the role of investor discussion boards. *Venture Capital, 21*(4), 327–352.

Kleinert, S., Volkmann, C., & Grünhagen, M. (2020). Third-party signals in equity crowdfunding: The role of prior financing. *Small Business Economics, 54*(1), 341–365.

Lim, J. Y.-K., & Busenitz, L. W. (2020). Evolving human capital of entrepreneurs in an equity crowdfunding era. *Journal of Small Business Management, 58*(1), 106–129.

Li, X., Tang, Y., Yang, N., Ren, R., Zheng, H., & Zhou, H. (2016). The value of information disclosure and lead investor in equity-based crowdfunding: An exploratory empirical study. *Nankai Business Review International.*

Löher, J., Schneck, S., & Werner, A. (2018). A research note on entrepreneurs' financial commitment and crowdfunding success. *Venture Capital, 20*(3), 309–322.

Lukkarinen, A., Teich, J. E., Wallenius, H., & Wallenius, J. (2016). Success drivers of online equity crowdfunding campaigns. *Decision Support Systems, 87*, 26–38.

Malaga, R., Mamonov, S., & Rosenblum, J. (2018). Gender difference in equity crowdfunding: An exploratory analysis. *International Journal of Gender and Entrepreneurship, 10*(4), 332–343.

Mamonov, S., & Malaga, R. (2019). Success factors in title ii equity crowdfunding in the united states. *Venture Capital, 21*(2–3), 223–241.

Meoli, M., & Vismara, S. (2021). Information manipulation in equity crowdfunding markets. *Journal of Corporate Finance, 67*, 101866.

Motylska-Kuzma, A. (2018). Crowdfunding and sustainable development. *Sustainability, 10*(12). https://doi.org/10.3390/su10124650

Nitani, M., Riding, A., & He, B. (2019). On equity crowdfunding: Investor rationality and success factors. *Venture Capital, 21*(2–3), 243–272.

Piva, E., & Rossi-Lamastra, C. (2018). Human capital signals and entrepreneurs' success in equity crowdfunding. *Small Business Economics, 51*(3), 667–686.

Ralcheva, A., & Roosenboom, P. (2020). Forecasting success in equity crowdfunding. *Small Business Economics, 55*(1), 39–56.

Shafi, K. (2021). Investors' evaluation criteria in equity crowdfunding. *Small Business Economics, 56*(1), 3–37.

Signori, A., & Vismara, S. (2018). Does success bring success? the post-offering lives of equity-crowdfunded firms. *Journal of Corporate Finance, 50*, 575–591.

Vismara, S. (2016). Equity retention and social network theory in equity crowdfunding. *Small Business Economics, 46*(4), 579–590.

Vismara, S. (2018). Information cascades among investors in equity crowdfunding. *Entrepreneurship Theory and Practice, 42*(3), 467–497.

Vismara, S. (2019). Sustainability in equity crowdfunding. *Technological Forecasting and Social Change, 141*, 98–106.

Vrontis, D., Christofi, M., Battisti, E., & Graziano, E. A. (2020). Intellectual capital, knowledge sharing and equity crowdfunding. *Journal of Intellectual Capital*.

Vulkan, N., Astebro, T., & Sierra, M. F. (2016). Equity crowdfunding: A new phenomena. *Journal of Business Venturing Insights, 5*, 37–49.

Walthoff-Borm, X., Vanacker, T. R., & Collewaert, V. (2018). Equity crowdfunding, shareholder structures, and firm performance. *Corporate Governance: An International Review, 26*(5), 314–330.

CHAPTER 6

# Empirical Results

**Abstract** This section provides the main empirical results obtained from the analysis. It contains both a descriptive overview of the samples, together with an exploratory analysis (univariate statistics, *t*-tests), and an inferential analysis on the observations, namely multivariate regressions. Lastly, the last subsections also provide analysis from both country-level and platform-level perspectives.

**Keywords** Findings · Information dissemination · Campaign success · Exploratory analysis · Institutional isomorphism · Investors' behaviour · Wisdom-of-crowds

The data mining procedure ended up selecting 24 variables: one variable (the binary variable Y1, campaign success) has been uniquely used as dependent variable; the remaining 23 variables have been used as independent ones, grouped in cluster as shown by Table 5.1 of the precedent chapter. Remember that, when compared vis-a-vis with existing literature, they are Data typology B of Fig. 5.1.



F. J. Mazzocchini and C. Lucarelli, *Investors' Preferences in Financing New Ventures*,
https://doi.org/10.1007/978-3-031-30058-5_6

## 6.1 Description of the Sample

In this section, we offer a sketch of how much of these 24 variables have been obtained for each specific platform. Table 6.1 offers a visual comparison of data obtained from the data mining procedure to compute metrics of dependent (Y) and clusters of independent variables (Ks). Note that to allow a meaningful comparison, we considered the maximum amount of available data for the overall sample of platforms (as shown in Table 5.1): they are $n = 5$ for metrics of dependent (Y), $n = 6$ for group of independent variables (K1), $n = 7$ for group of independent variables (K2), $n = 5$ for group of independent variables (K3) and $n = 5$[1] for group of independent variables (K4). Therefore, axes of the radars plotted in Table 6.1 are from a minimum of 0 (no variable detected for that cluster in that specific platform) to a maximum of 1 (100% of variables detected for that group in that specific platform).

Immediately, first evidence of our empirical research is pacific: the public information disclosed by ECF platforms, across countries, is very different, in terms of both typologies and details for each typology, as it is going to be discussed in the Sect. 6.4.1.

A complementary information useful to sketch the overall feature of data obtained with the data mining procedure is offered by Table 6.2 which counts the number of campaigns detected for each platform, within the same observation period. Again, this number is very distinctive, indicating a various intensity of activity across ECF platforms, going from the minimum of 48 campaigns resulting for the Italian 200Crowd, up to the maximum of 769 campaigns appearing in the British Seedrs.

For this reason, to comment properly the summary figures resulting from the data mining extraction, we re-order the ECF platforms: from the mere initial alphabetic order, since now we order platforms splitting the sample into two subgroups: on the one hand, the platforms from countries not belonging to the European Union (i.e., the US Crowdfunder and the British Crowdcube and Seedrs), and on the other hand, the platforms from countries who are members of the European

[1] Remember that 4 of these variables may be used also as dependent variables, depending on the model estimated. So, for this descripted evidence they are counted double, both in the Y and K4 group of potential variables.

**Table 6.1** Cross-platforms comparison of available data to compute metrics of dependent (Y) and groups of independent variables (Ks)

| 200Crowd<br>Italy | Companisto<br>Germany | Crowdcube<br>United Kingdom | Crowdfunder<br>United States | Fundedbyme<br>Sweden |
|---|---|---|---|---|
| 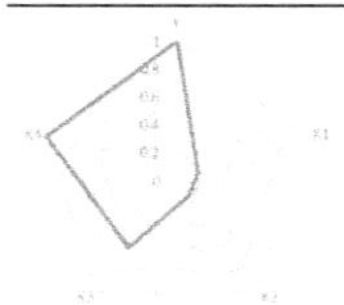 | 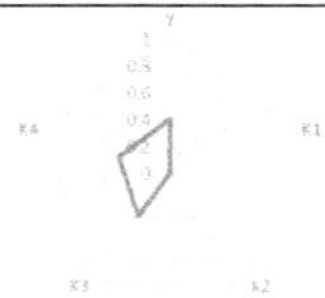 | 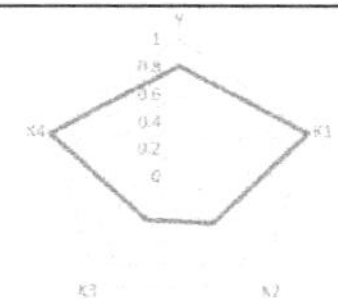 | 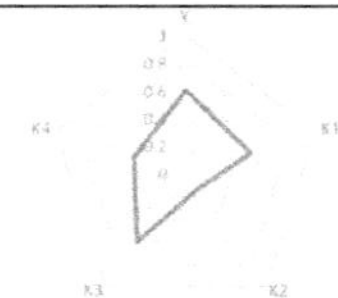 | 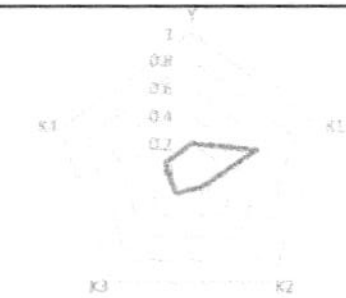 |
| **Invesdor**<br>**Finland** | **Mamacrowd**<br>**Italy** | **Opstart**<br>**Italy** | **Seedrs**<br>**United Kingdom** | **Sowefund**<br>**France** |
| 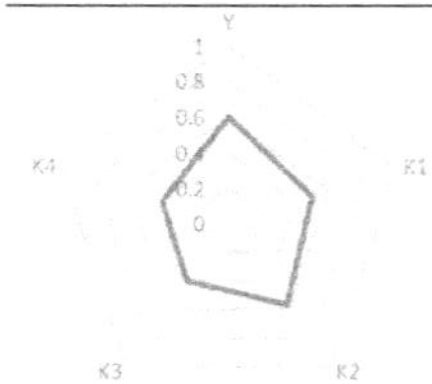 | 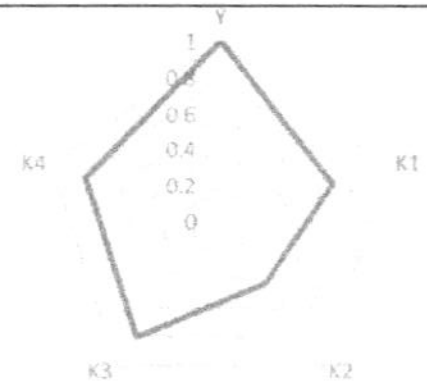 | 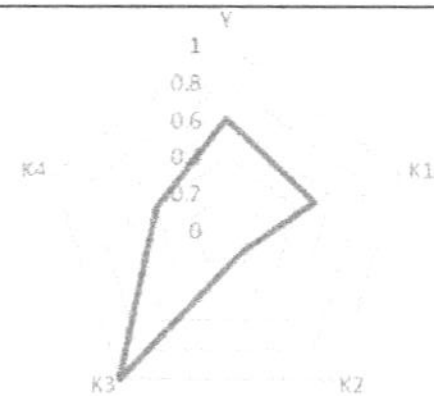 | 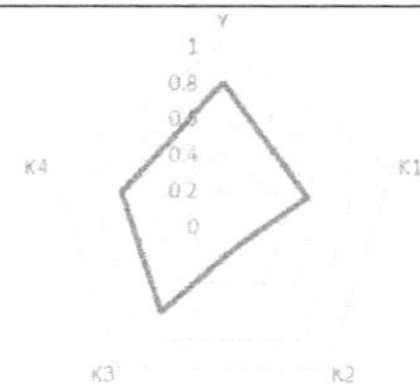 | 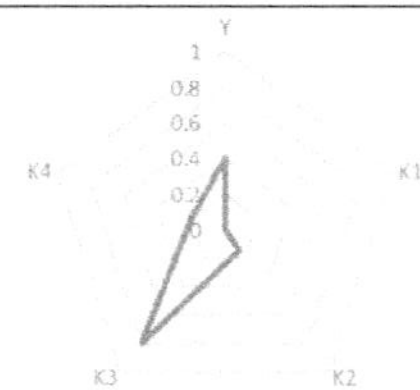 |

**Table 6.2** Campaigns for platform

| | | *200Crowd* | *Companisto* | *Crowdcube* | *Crowdfunder* | *Fundedbyme* | *Invesdor* | *Mamacrowd* | *Opstart* | *Seedrs* | *Sowefund* |
|---|---|---|---|---|---|---|---|---|---|---|---|
| Y1 | Campaign success | 48 | | 314 | 134 | | 146 | 97 | 80 | 741 | 94 |
| Y2/K4 | Percentage raised | 48 | | 314 | 134 | | 146 | 97 | 80 | 741 | 57 |
| Y3/K4 | Capital raised | 48 | 110 | 312 | 134 | 197 | 140 | 97 | 80 | 748 | |
| Y4/K4 | Number of investors | 48 | 101 | 314 | | | | 97 | | 132 | |
| Y5/K4 | Professional investors | 48 | | | | | | 97 | | | |
| K1 | Entrepreneur age | | | 309 | | | | | | | |
| K1 | Entrepreneur gender | | | 312 | 264 | | 121 | 97 | 80 | | |
| K1 | Entrepreneur experience | | | 312 | | | | | | | |
| K1 | Equity retention | 48 | | 307 | | 195 | | 97 | | 610 | |
| K1 | Social media presence | | | 314 | 288 | 213 | 153 | 97 | 80 | 769 | |
| K1 | Social media count | | | 314 | 288 | 213 | 153 | 97 | 80 | 769 | |
| K2 | Financial forecast (year) | | | | | | 129 | | | | |

| | | *200Crowd* | *Companisto* | *Crowdcube* | *Crowdfunder* | *Fundedbyme* | *Invesdor* | *Mamacrowd* | *Opstart* | *Seedrs* | *Sowefund* |
|---|---|---|---|---|---|---|---|---|---|---|---|
| K2 | Financial forecast | | | | | | 124 | | | | |
| K2 | Equity | | | | | | | 97 | | | |
| K2 | Pre-money | 48 | | 303 | | | | 97 | 80 | | |
| K2 | Outstanding shares | | | | | | 127 | | | | |
| K2 | Firm location | | | 313 | 287 | 213 | 153 | 97 | | 273 | 96 |
| K2 | Firm maturity | | | 313 | | | | | | | |
| K3 | Share price | | 107 | | 134 | | | 97 | 80 | 423 | 104 |
| K3 | Min. funding target | 48 | | 312 | 134 | | 146 | 97 | 80 | 675 | 97 |
| K3 | Max. funding target | 48 | | | | | | 97 | 80 | | 81 |
| K3 | Max. retail investment | | | | | | | | 79 | | |
| K3 | COVID period | 48 | 111 | 314 | 288 | 213 | 153 | 97 | 80 | 769 | 104 |
| K4 | Interested investors | 48 | | 224 | | | | | | | |
| | Campaigns | 48 | 111 | 314 | 288 | 213 | 153 | 97 | 80 | 769 | 104 |

Union (i.e., the French Sowefund, the German Companisto, the Italian 200Crowd, Mamacrow and Opstart, the Swedish Fundedbyme and the Finnish Invesdor).

## 6.2 Exploratory Analysis

From this section onwards, sampled platforms have been ordered into two groups: three platforms from countries not belonging to the European Union (i.e., the US Crowdfunder and the British Crowdcube and Seedrs), and seven platforms from countries who are members of the European Union (i.e., the French Sowefund, the German Companisto, the Swedish FundedByMe and the Finnish Invesdor, the Italian 200Crowd, Mamacrow and Opstart). Under this latter sub-group, we can distinguish two platforms of Scandinavia countries and three from Italy. This expression of different platforms belonging to the same geographical area/country allows to consider some area/country regularities.

In fact, with regard to platforms from Anglo-Saxon area (the US and the UK), Table 6.3 indicates which features result as significantly different, in terms of the mean value of the corresponding variable.[2] Precisely, the US and the UK campaigns, even if it would seem that they collect an inferior Y2—i.e., percentage of capital raised—in the truth they raise higher capital in absolute terms (Y3) with higher number of investors (Y4).

This would mean that projects asking funding with ECF are bigger/valuable than the average in EU platforms, and this appears to be coherent with the statistically higher pre-money and higher minimum funding target, even if firms appear younger (lower firm maturity) and more focused on money they ask, shown by lower max. funding target. ECF appear much more developed in terms of ECF acquaintance of investors, with incredibly higher Interested investors by campaign, even if with statistically lower Digital media social network, in terms of inferior presence of social media information disclosed within each campaign, and their variety (Social media count).

In this section, we also report tables of detailed summaries statistics for each platform. Notably, we follow the order of the above-mentioned area/country rule. Here, we need to point out that this information

[2] Tables 6.3, 6.9, and 6.12 show uniquely variables that appear statistically different from T-Student tests.

**Table 6.3** Variables of the US-UK platform statistically different from platforms of EU countries

| | *Group* | *Obs* | *Mean* | *Std.Err* | *Std.Dev* | *[95% Conf. Interval]* | |
|---|---|---|---|---|---|---|---|
| Y2 Percentage raised | Rest of the sample | 428.00 | 2.21 | 0.46 | 9.59 | 1.30 | 3.12 |
| | The US-UK platforms | 1189.00 | 1.31 | 0.03 | 1.05 | 1.25 | 1.37 |
| | Combined | 1617.00 | 1.55 | 0.13 | 5.03 | 1.31 | 1.80 |
| Y3 Capital raised | Rest of the sample | 685.00 | 11.19 | 0.11 | 2.96 | 10.97 | 11.42 |
| | The US-UK platforms | 1194.00 | 12.20 | 0.08 | 2.76 | 12.05 | 12.36 |
| | Combined | 1879.00 | 11.84 | 0.07 | 2.88 | 11.71 | 11.97 |
| Y4 Number of investors | Rest of the sample | 253.00 | 336.39 | 25.66 | 408.16 | 285.85 | 386.93 |
| | The US-UK platforms | 446.00 | 456.89 | 35.15 | 742.27 | 387.82 | 525.97 |
| | Combined | 699.00 | 413.28 | 24.36 | 644.02 | 365.45 | 461.11 |
| Social media presence | Rest of the sample | 543.00 | 0.73 | 0.02 | 0.45 | 0.69 | 0.76 |
| | The US-UK platforms | 1371.00 | 0.37 | 0.01 | 0.48 | 0.34 | 0.39 |
| | Combined | 1914.00 | 0.47 | 0.01 | 0.50 | 0.45 | 0.49 |
| Social media count | Rest of the sample | 543.00 | 1.00 | 0.04 | 0.86 | 0.93 | 1.07 |
| | The US-UK platforms | 1371.00 | 0.42 | 0.02 | 0.60 | 0.39 | 0.45 |
| | Combined | 1914.00 | 0.58 | 0.02 | 0.73 | 0.55 | 0.61 |
| Pre-money | Rest of the sample | 232.00 | 14.33 | 0.08 | 1.23 | 14.17 | 14.49 |
| | The US-UK platforms | 315.00 | 15.10 | 0.06 | 1.12 | 14.97 | 15.22 |
| | Combined | 547.00 | 14.77 | 0.05 | 1.22 | 14.67 | 14.88 |
| Firm maturity | Rest of the sample | 391.00 | 5.86 | 0.06 | 1.12 | 5.75 | 5.97 |
| | The US-UK platforms | 567.00 | 3.64 | 0.13 | 3.03 | 3.39 | 3.89 |
| | Combined | 958.00 | 4.54 | 0.09 | 2.67 | 4.38 | 4.71 |

(continued)

**Table 6.3** (continued)

| | *Group* | *Obs* | *Mean* | *Std.Err* | *Std.Dev* | *[95% Conf. Interval]* | |
|---|---|---|---|---|---|---|---|
| Min. funding target | Rest of the sample | 471.00 | 12.02 | 0.05 | 1.00 | 11.93 | 12.11 |
| | The US-UK platforms | 1121.00 | 12.49 | 0.04 | 1.35 | 12.41 | 12.57 |
| | Combined | 1592.00 | 12.35 | 0.03 | 1.28 | 12.29 | 12.42 |
| Max. funding target | Rest of the sample | 82.00 | 12.94 | 0.05 | 0.43 | 12.85 | 13.04 |
| | The US-UK platforms | 225.00 | 12.73 | 0.06 | 0.87 | 12.61 | 12.84 |
| | Combined | 307.00 | 12.78 | 0.04 | 0.78 | 12.70 | 12.87 |
| Interested investors | Rest of the sample | 87.00 | 45.99 | 9.20 | 85.84 | 27.69 | 64.28 |
| | The US-UK platforms | 234.00 | 1115.30 | 98.81 | 1511.43 | 920.63 | 1309.96 |
| | Combined | 321.00 | 825.48 | 76.77 | 1375.48 | 674.44 | 976.52 |

includes figures of variables (marked with #), belonging to the 24 selected ones, but that are very occasional withing the campaigns belonging to a given platform. This intra-platform scarcity of data forced us to exclude them in the following multivariate estimates.[3] Then, the column *t*-test indicates if the mean value for a given variable is significantly superior (>), significantly inferior (<) or not statistically different (≈) from the corresponding mean value of the same variable computed in the rest of the sample. For eight variables, this test is not applicable (NA) because the variable is present only in one platform: Entreprenur age, Entrepreneur experience and Firm maturity are present only in Crowdcube; Financial forecast, Financial forecast (year) and Outstanding shares are present only in Investor, Equity is present only in Mamacrowd, Max. retail investment is present only in Opstart. Note that the § stands to indicate that the variable is expressed in natural log (Table 6.4).

[3] Note that estimations by platform are carried out on the complete dataset of variables available. The inclusion of a variable with very few observations for that platform, would have endangered the whole estimation. For the sake of significance of multivariate analysis, we omit this kind of items in estimations.

**Table 6.4** Summary statistics Crowdfunder—US

| | | *Obs* | t-*test* | *Mean* | *Median* | *Std.Dev* | *Min* | *Max* |
|---|---|---|---|---|---|---|---|---|
| Y1 | Campaign success | 134 | < | 0.13 | 0.00 | 0.33 | 0.00 | 1 |
| Y2/K4 | Percentage raised | 134 | < | 0.52 | 0.05 | 1.52 | 0.00 | 15 |
| Y3/K4 | Capital raised§ | 134 | < | 8.31 | 10.90 | 5.98 | 0.00 | 16 |
| K1 | Entrepreneur gender | 264 | < | 0.13 | 0.00 | 0.34 | 0.00 | 1 |
| K1 | Social media presence | 288 | < | 0.38 | 0.00 | 0.48 | 0.00 | 1 |
| K1 | Social media count | 288 | ≈ | 0.57 | 0.00 | 0.82 | 0.00 | 3 |
| K2 | Firm location | 287 | ≈ | 0.84 | 1.00 | 0.37 | 0.00 | 1 |
| K3 | Share price§ | 134 | > | 8.40 | 8.43 | 1.90 | 2.24 | 14 |
| K3 | Min. funding target§ | 134 | > | 13.76 | 13.72 | 1.45 | 7.43 | 17 |
| K3 | COVID period | 288 | NA | 0.16 | 0.00 | 0.36 | 0.00 | 1 |
| | Observations | 288 | | | | | | |

Among the Anglo-Saxon platforms, it is noticeable that the US platform Crowdfunder appears showing statistically lower (relative) metrics for campaign success and percentage raised, but also lower capital raised in absolute terms. This is to deduce that the higher capital raised in absolute terms shown as the whole Anglo-Saxon area of Table 6.3 is entirely due to this feature within the UK platforms, both Crowdcube (see Table 6.5) and Seedrs (see Table 6.6).

Tables from 6.7 to 6.15 from contain summary statistics of platforms belonging to EU member states. Since the preliminary and visual description shown by Table 6.1, French and German platforms appear, in general, less informative, presenting few data obtained by web with the data mining procedure.

The French Sowefund (see Table 6.7), with 104 campaigns collected in the observed period, shows projects with inferior Y1 campaign success, mostly France-based (Firm location) but with high financing demand (Share price, Min. funding target, Max. funding target variables featured by higher average amount than the remaining platforms).

The German platform (see Table 6.8), with 111 campaigns for the observed period, offer even less public information than the French one, but with statistically higher Y2 capital raised, higher Y4 number of investors and higher Share price.

Then, we report statistics for the Sweden and Finnish platforms, as expression of the regional Scandinavian geographical area (see Table 6.9).

**Table 6.5** Summary statistics Crowdcube—UK

| | | *Obs* | t-*test* | *Mean* | *Median* | *Std.Dev* | *Min* | *Max* |
|---|---|---|---|---|---|---|---|---|
| Y1 | Campaign success | 314 | ≈ | 0.73 | 1.00 | 0.45 | 0.00 | 1 |
| Y2/K4 | Percentage raised | 314 | ≈ | 1.59 | 1.28 | 1.30 | 0.20 | 10 |
| Y3/K4 | Capital raised§ | 312 | > | 12.51 | 12.38 | 1.17 | 9.88 | 16 |
| Y4/K4 | Number of investors | 314 | > | 490.05 | 273.00 | 857.62 | 27.00 | 10,363 |
| K1 | Entrepreneur age | 309 | NA | 45.29 | 45.00 | 11.09 | 23.00 | 76 |
| K1 | Entrepreneur gender | 312 | > | 0.22 | 0.00 | 0.42 | 0.00 | 1 |
| K1 | Entrepreneur experience | 312 | NA | 3.68 | 3.00 | 2.77 | 0.00 | 17 |
| K1 | Equity retention | 307 | > | 91.13 | 92.09 | 4.73 | 73.14 | 98 |
| K1 | Social media presence | 314 | < | 0.36 | 0.00 | 0.48 | 0.00 | 1 |
| K1 | Social media count | 314 | < | 0.35 | 0.00 | 0.48 | 0.00 | 1 |
| K2 | Pre-money§ | 303 | > | 15.07 | 14.91 | 1.12 | 12.72 | 19 |
| K2 | Firm location | 313 | < | 0.83 | 1.00 | 0.37 | 0.00 | 1 |
| K2 | Firm maturity | 313 | NA | 4.65 | 4.00 | 3.23 | 0.00 | 22 |
| K3 | Min. funding target§ | 312 | ≈ | 12.30 | 12.21 | 0.91 | 9.21 | 15 |
| K3 | COVID period | 314 | NA | 0.19 | 0.00 | 0.39 | 0.00 | 1 |
| K4 | Interested investors | 224 | > | 1127.59 | 677.50 | 1540.53 | 19.00 | 16,836 |
| | Observations | 314 | | | | | | |

It appears that this area shows higher expressions of success of ECF projects, both in relative (Y1 Campaign success) and absolute terms (Y3 Capital raised), even if projects, frequently located outside the Scandinavian region (lower values of Firm location), seem to show high finance demanding (statistically higher Min. funding target). Interestingly, Social media presence and distribution among different digital media (Social media count) is higher than the average of the rest of sample, even if number of Interested investors appear statistically lower (Tables 6.10 and 6.11).

**Table 6.6** Summary statistics Seedrs—UK

| | | *Obs* | t-*test* | *Mean* | *Median* | *Std.Dev* | *Min* | *Max* |
|---|---|---|---|---|---|---|---|---|
| Y1 | Campaign success | 741 | > | 0.87 | 1.00 | 0.34 | 0.00 | 1 |
| Y2/K4 | Percentage raised | 741 | ≈ | 1.34 | 1.15 | 0.70 | 0.00 | 9 |
| Y3/K4 | Capital raised§ | 748 | > | 12.77 | 12.66 | 1.48 | 6.82 | 17 |
| Y4/K4 | Number of investors | 132 | ≈ | 378.02 | 266.00 | 324.57 | 38.00 | 1624 |
| K1 | Entrepreneur gender | 1 | | | | | | |
| K1 | Equity retention | 610 | ≈ | 90.43 | 91.67 | 6.11 | 60.00 | 100 |
| K1 | Social media presence | 769 | < | 0.37 | 0.00 | 0.48 | 0.00 | 1 |
| K1 | Social media count | 769 | < | 0.39 | 0.00 | 0.53 | 0.00 | 3 |
| K2 | Pre-money# | 12 | > | 15.81 | 15.60 | 0.94 | 14.63 | 18 |
| K2 | Firm location | 273 | ≈ | 0.87 | 1.00 | 0.34 | 0.00 | 1 |
| K3 | Share price§ | 423 | < | 2.19 | 2.24 | 1.31 | 0.01 | 10 |
| K3 | Min. funding target§ | 675 | ≈ | 12.33 | 12.32 | 1.37 | 6.65 | 16 |
| K3 | COVID period | 769 | NA | 0.16 | 0.00 | 0.37 | 0.00 | 1 |
| K4 | Interested investors# | 10 | ≈ | 839.80 | 889.00 | 499.73 | 135.00 | 1595 |
| | Observations | 769 | | | | | | |

**Table 6.7** Summary statistics Sowefund—France

| | | *Obs* | t-*test* | *Mean* | *Median* | *Std.Dev* | *Min* | *Max* |
|---|---|---|---|---|---|---|---|---|
| Y1 | Campaign success | 94 | < | 0.39 | 0.00 | 0.49 | 0.00 | 1 |
| K1 | Entrepreneur gender# | 33 | ≈ | 0.12 | 0.00 | 0.33 | 0.00 | 1 |
| K2 | Firm location | 96 | > | 0.96 | 1.00 | 0.20 | 0.00 | 1 |
| K3 | Share price§ | 104 | > | 5.01 | 4.62 | 1.10 | 4.62 | 11 |
| K3 | Min. funding target§ | 97 | > | 12.79 | 12.90 | 0.67 | 10.82 | 16 |
| K3 | Max. funding target§ | 81 | > | 12.94 | 13.12 | 0.43 | 11.51 | 14 |
| K3 | COVID period | 104 | NA | 0.13 | 0.00 | 0.34 | 0.00 | 1 |
| | Observations | 104 | | | | | | |

**Table 6.8** Summary statistics Companisto—Germany

| | | *Obs* | t-*test* | *Mean* | *Median* | *Std.Dev* | *Min* | *Max* |
|---|---|---|---|---|---|---|---|---|
| Y3/K4 | Capital raised§ | 110 | > | 12.65 | 12.61 | 1.06 | 10.34 | 15 |
| Y4/K4 | Number of investors | 101 | > | 677.86 | 627.00 | 396.95 | 47.00 | 2276 |
| K3 | Share price§ | 107 | > | 6.20 | 6.18 | 0.72 | 4.80 | 9 |
| K3 | COVID period | 111 | NA | 0.16 | 0.00 | 0.37 | 0.00 | 1 |
| | Observations | 111 | | | | | | |

**Table 6.9** Variables of Sweden and Finnish platforms statistically different from the rest of the sample

| | *Group* | *Obs* | *Mean* | *Std.Err* | *Std.Dev* | *[95% Conf. Interval]* | |
|---|---|---|---|---|---|---|---|
| Y1 Campaign success | Rest of the sample | 1508.00 | 0.74 | 0.01 | 0.44 | 0.71 | 0.76 |
| | Scandinavian platforms | 182.00 | 0.89 | 0.02 | 0.31 | 0.84 | 0.94 |
| | Combined | 1690.00 | 0.75 | 0.01 | 0.43 | 0.73 | 0.77 |
| Y3 Capital raised | Rest of the sample | 1542.00 | 11.78 | 0.08 | 3.12 | 11.62 | 11.93 |
| | Scandinavian platforms | 337.00 | 12.10 | 0.07 | 1.20 | 11.97 | 12.23 |
| | Combined | 1879.00 | 11.84 | 0.07 | 2.88 | 11.71 | 11.97 |
| Social media presence | Rest of the sample | 1548.00 | 0.41 | 0.01 | 0.49 | 0.39 | 0.43 |
| | Scandinavian platforms | 366.00 | 0.72 | 0.02 | 0.45 | 0.67 | 0.76 |
| | Combined | 1914.00 | 0.47 | 0.01 | 0.50 | 0.45 | 0.49 |
| Social media count | Rest of the sample | 1548.00 | 0.53 | 0.02 | 0.76 | 0.50 | 0.57 |
| | Scandinavian platforms | 366.00 | 0.79 | 0.03 | 0.56 | 0.73 | 0.84 |
| | Combined | 1914.00 | 0.58 | 0.02 | 0.73 | 0.55 | 0.61 |
| Firm location | Rest of the sample | 1066.00 | 0.87 | 0.01 | 0.34 | 0.85 | 0.89 |
| | Scandinavian platforms | 366.00 | 0.79 | 0.02 | 0.41 | 0.75 | 0.83 |
| | Combined | 1432.00 | 0.85 | 0.01 | 0.36 | 0.83 | 0.87 |
| Min. funding target | Rest of the sample | 1443.00 | 12.38 | 0.03 | 1.29 | 12.31 | 12.44 |
| | Scandinavian platforms | 149.00 | 12.11 | 0.09 | 1.05 | 11.94 | 12.28 |
| | Combined | 1592.00 | 12.35 | 0.03 | 1.28 | 12.29 | 12.42 |
| Interested investors | Rest of the sample | 282.00 | 932.62 | 85.45 | 1435.02 | 764.41 | 1100.83 |
| | Scandinavian platforms | 39.00 | 50.82 | 9.14 | 57.08 | 32.32 | 69.32 |
| | Combined | 321.00 | 825.48 | 76.77 | 1375.48 | 674.44 | 976.52 |

**Table 6.10** Summary statistics Fundedbyme—Sweden

| | | *Obs* | t-*test* | *Mean* | *Median* | *Std.Dev* | *Min* | *Max* |
|---|---|---|---|---|---|---|---|---|
| Y1 | Campaign success# | 1 | NA | 1 | | | | |
| Y3/K4 | Capital raised§ | 197 | ≈ | 11.80 | 11.74 | 1.10 | 8.61 | 15 |
| Y4/K4 | Number of investors# | 3 | ≈ | 54.67 | 39.00 | 28.01 | 38.00 | 87 |
| K1 | Equity retention | 195 | ≈ | 90.79 | 92.88 | 8.17 | 25.07 | 99 |
| K1 | Social media presence | 213 | > | 0.78 | 1.00 | 0.41 | 0.00 | 1 |
| K1 | Social media count | 213 | > | 0.91 | 1.00 | 0.58 | 0.00 | 2 |
| K2 | Firm location | 213 | < | 0.74 | 1.00 | 0.44 | 0.00 | 1 |
| K3 | Share price# | 2 | ≈ | 4.64 | 4.64 | | 4.64 | 5 |
| K3 | Min. funding target# | 3 | ≈ | 11.54 | 11.49 | 1.56 | 10.00 | 13 |
| K3 | COVID period | 213 | NA | 0.17 | 0.00 | 0.38 | 0.00 | 1 |
| | Observations | 213 | | | | | | |

Finally, it is relevant to show the Italian case, with three ECF platforms (200Crowd, Mamacrowd and Opstart). Since the preliminary and visual description shown by Table 6.1, Italian platforms appear, in general, very informative, presenting a lot of web data collectable with data mining procedures. Interestingly, it appears that the Italian ECF case is quite distinguishable, compared to the remaining sample, with the long list of variables that are statistically different, as shown by Table 6.12. First of all, almost all the Italian platforms show all the four metrics for ECF success (Y1 Campaign success, Y2 Percentage raised, Y3 Capital raised, Y4 Number of investors) but the relative measures are higher than the average of the rest of the sample, whereas the absolute measures are lower, indicating that Italian ECF projects are of smaller values (see coherently the Pre-money, Min. funding target and Max. funding target values that are lower, even if the Share price is higher than the average of the rest of the sample). Moreover, ECF projects are mostly presented by male entrepreneurs (Entrepreneur gender variable) and business activities are mostly in Italy (Firm location). Finally, with similarities with the Scandinavia case, Social media presence and distribution among different digital media (Social media count) is higher than the average of the rest of the sample, even if number of Interested investors appear statistically lower. This means just an opposite situation compared to what we found in the UK case (Tables 6.13, 6.14, and 6.15).

**Table 6.11** Summary statistics Invesdor—Finland

| | | *Obs* | t-*test* | *Mean* | *Median* | *Std.Dev* | *Min* | *Max* |
|---|---|---|---|---|---|---|---|---|
| Y1 | Campaign success | 146 | > | 0.86 | 1.00 | 0.35 | 0.00 | 1 |
| Y2/K4 | Percentage raised | 146 | ≈ | 1.78 | 1.46 | 1.33 | 0.14 | 10 |
| Y3/K4 | Capital raised§ | 140 | > | 12.53 | 12.55 | 1.21 | 9.32 | 15 |
| Y4/K4 | Number of investors# | 4 | ≈ | 355.75 | 354.00 | 281.94 | 27.00 | 688 |
| K1 | Entrepreneur gender | 121 | ≈ | 0.19 | 0.00 | 0.39 | 0.00 | 1 |
| K1 | Equity retention | 1 | NA | | | | | |
| K1 | Social media presence | 153 | > | 0.63 | 1.00 | 0.49 | 0.00 | 1 |
| K1 | Social media count | 153 | ≈ | 0.62 | 1.00 | 0.49 | 0.00 | 1 |
| K2 | Financial forecast§ | 124 | NA | 14.31 | 14.44 | 1.35 | 9.39 | 18 |
| K2 | Financial forecast (year) | 129 | NA | 2017.59 | 2018.00 | 1.93 | 2014.00 | 2021 |
| K2 | Outstanding shares | 127 | NA | 1,557,491.44 | 101,208.00 | 5,498,528.58 | 500.00 | 54,071,764 |
| K2 | Firm location | 153 | ≈ | 0.86 | 1.00 | 0.35 | 0.00 | 1 |
| K3 | Min. funding target§ | 146 | < | 12.12 | 12.21 | 1.04 | 9.90 | 14 |
| K3 | Pre-money# | 7 | ≈ | 14.84 | 14.85 | 0.29 | 14.50 | 15 |
| K3 | COVID period | 153 | NA | 0.22 | 0.00 | 0.42 | 0.00 | 1 |
| | Observations | 153 | | | | | | |

**Table 6.12** Variables of Italian platform statistically different from the rest of the sample

| | *Group* | *Obs* | *Mean* | *Std.Err* | *Std.Dev* | *[95% Conf. Interval]* | |
|---|---|---|---|---|---|---|---|
| Y1 Campaign success | Rest of the sample | 1465.00 | 0.74 | 0.01 | 0.44 | 0.72 | 0.76 |
| | Italian platforms | 225.00 | 0.83 | 0.03 | 0.38 | 0.78 | 0.88 |
| | Combined | 1690.00 | 0.75 | 0.01 | 0.43 | 0.73 | 0.77 |
| Y2 Percentage raised | Rest of the sample | 1392.00 | 1.31 | 0.03 | 1.11 | 1.25 | 1.37 |
| | Italian platforms | 225.00 | 3.05 | 0.87 | 13.12 | 1.32 | 4.77 |
| | Combined | 1617.00 | 1.55 | 0.13 | 5.03 | 1.31 | 1.80 |
| Y3 Capital raised | Rest of the sample | 1654.00 | 12.12 | 0.07 | 2.66 | 11.99 | 12.24 |
| | Italian platforms | 225.00 | 9.77 | 0.23 | 3.52 | 9.31 | 10.23 |
| | Combined | 1879.00 | 11.84 | 0.07 | 2.88 | 11.71 | 11.97 |
| Y4 Number of investors | Rest of the sample | 554.00 | 494.27 | 29.46 | 693.37 | 436.41 | 552.13 |
| | Italian platforms | 145.00 | 103.83 | 17.13 | 206.26 | 69.98 | 137.69 |
| | Combined | 699.00 | 413.28 | 24.36 | 644.02 | 365.45 | 461.11 |
| Entrepreneur gender | Rest of the sample | 731.00 | 0.18 | 0.01 | 0.38 | 0.15 | 0.21 |
| | Italian platforms | 177.00 | 0.10 | 0.02 | 0.30 | 0.05 | 0.14 |
| | Combined | 908.00 | 0.16 | 0.01 | 0.37 | 0.14 | 0.19 |
| Social media presence | Rest of the sample | 1737.00 | 0.44 | 0.01 | 0.50 | 0.42 | 0.46 |
| | Italian platforms | 177.00 | 0.74 | 0.03 | 0.44 | 0.67 | 0.81 |
| | Combined | 1914.00 | 0.47 | 0.01 | 0.50 | 0.45 | 0.49 |
| Social media count | Rest of the sample | 1737.00 | 0.50 | 0.01 | 0.61 | 0.47 | 0.52 |
| | Italian platforms | 177.00 | 1.44 | 0.09 | 1.16 | 1.26 | 1.61 |
| | Combined | 1914.00 | 0.58 | 0.02 | 0.73 | 0.55 | 0.61 |

(continued)

**Table 6.12** (continued)

| | *Group* | *Obs* | *Mean* | *Std.Err* | *Std.Dev* | *[95% Conf. Interval]* | |
|---|---|---|---|---|---|---|---|
| Pre-money | Rest of the sample | 322.00 | 15.09 | 0.06 | 1.11 | 14.97 | 15.21 |
| | Italian platforms | 225.00 | 14.32 | 0.08 | 1.24 | 14.15 | 14.48 |
| | combined | 547.00 | 14.77 | 0.05 | 1.22 | 14.67 | 14.88 |
| Firm location | Rest of the sample | 1335.00 | 0.84 | 0.01 | 0.37 | 0.82 | 0.86 |
| | Italian platforms | 97.00 | 1.00 | 0.00 | 0.00 | 1.00 | 1.00 |
| | Combined | 1432.00 | 0.85 | 0.01 | 0.36 | 0.83 | 0.87 |
| Share price | Rest of the sample | 781.00 | 4.17 | 0.10 | 2.79 | 3.98 | 4.37 |
| | Italian platforms | 177.00 | 6.18 | 0.08 | 1.07 | 6.02 | 6.34 |
| | Combined | 958.00 | 4.54 | 0.09 | 2.67 | 4.38 | 4.71 |
| Min. funding target | Rest of the sample | 1367.00 | 12.47 | 0.03 | 1.29 | 12.40 | 12.54 |
| | Italian platforms | 225.00 | 11.62 | 0.06 | 0.88 | 11.51 | 11.74 |
| | Combined | 1592.00 | 12.35 | 0.03 | 1.28 | 12.29 | 12.42 |
| Max. funding target | Rest of the sample | 82.00 | 12.94 | 0.05 | 0.43 | 12.85 | 13.04 |
| | Italian platforms | 225.00 | 12.73 | 0.06 | 0.87 | 12.61 | 12.84 |
| | Combined | 307.00 | 12.78 | 0.04 | 0.78 | 12.70 | 12.87 |
| Interested investors | Rest of the sample | 273.00 | 963.23 | 87.63 | 1447.96 | 790.70 | 1135.76 |
| | Italian platforms | 48.00 | 42.06 | 15.01 | 103.99 | 11.87 | 72.26 |
| | Combined | 321.00 | 825.48 | 76.77 | 1375.48 | 674.44 | 976.52 |

## 6.3 Determinants of ECF Success

### *6.3.1 Country-Level Analysis*

Recall that estimations in this paper investigate what could bring to an ECF success, given that this implies engagement of the crowd of investors. The ECF success can be expressed in various forms, based also on the different information broadcasted by platforms. Coherently, the dependent variable in our models ends up in five expressions of success,

**Table 6.13** Summary statistics 200Crowd—Italy

| | | *Obs* | t-*test* | *Mean* | *Median* | *Std.Dev* | *Min* | *Max* |
|---|---|---|---|---|---|---|---|---|
| Y1 | Campaign success | 48 | ≈ | 0.77 | 1.00 | 0.42 | 0.00 | 1 |
| Y2/K4 | Percentage raised | 48 | ≈ | 1.62 | 1.49 | 1.11 | 0.00 | 4 |
| Y3/K4 | Capital raised§ | 48 | ≈ | 11.86 | 11.92 | 1.33 | 6.91 | 15 |
| Y4/K4 | Number of investors | 48 | < | 66.35 | 30.00 | 152.19 | 2.00 | 1060 |
| Y5/K4 | Professional investors | 48 | ≈ | 0.77 | 1.00 | 0.42 | 0.00 | 1 |
| K1 | Equity retention | 48 | ≈ | 90.20 | 92.26 | 6.24 | 75.00 | 98 |
| K2 | Pre-money§ | 48 | ≈ | 14.65 | 14.51 | 0.87 | 13.02 | 18 |
| K3 | Min. funding target§ | 48 | < | 11.79 | 11.70 | 0.68 | 10.82 | 14 |
| K3 | Max. funding target§ | 48 | ≈ | 12.70 | 12.61 | 0.69 | 11.51 | 15 |
| K3 | COVID period | 48 | NA | 0.15 | 0.00 | 0.36 | 0.00 | 1 |
| K4 | Interested investors | 48 | < | 42.06 | 23.00 | 103.99 | 1.00 | 729 |
| | Observations | 48 | | | | | | |

**Table 6.14** Summary statistics Mamacrowd—Italy

| | | *Obs* | t-*test* | *Mean* | *Median* | *Std.Dev* | *Min* | *Max* |
|---|---|---|---|---|---|---|---|---|
| Y1 | Campaign success | 97 | > | 0.85 | 1.00 | 0.36 | 0.00 | 1 |
| Y2/K4 | Percentage raised | 97 | > | 2.20 | 1.83 | 1.71 | 0.00 | 10 |
| Y3/K4 | Capital raised§ | 97 | < | 7.15 | 5.81 | 3.82 | 0.00 | 15 |
| Y4/K4 | Number of investors | 97 | < | 122.38 | 72.00 | 226.78 | 0.00 | 2080 |
| Y5/K4 | Professional investors | 97 | ≈ | 0.85 | 1.00 | 0.36 | 0.00 | 1 |
| K1 | Entrepreneur gender | 97 | < | 0.11 | 0.00 | 0.32 | 0.00 | 1 |
| K1 | Equity retention | 97 | ≈ | 90.75 | 94.59 | 15.27 | 2.00 | 99 |
| K1 | Social media presence | 97 | > | 0.91 | 1.00 | 0.29 | 0.00 | 1 |
| K1 | Social media count | 97 | > | 2.10 | 2.00 | 1.06 | 0.00 | 4 |
| K2 | Equity§ | 97 | NA | 9.54 | 9.32 | 1.79 | 4.62 | 15 |
| K2 | Pre-money§ | 97 | > | 14.52 | 14.56 | 1.37 | 6.91 | 16 |
| K2 | Firm location | 97 | < | 1.00 | 1.00 | 0.00 | 1.00 | 1 |
| K3 | Share price§ | 97 | > | 6.23 | 6.22 | 0.71 | 4.62 | 10 |
| K3 | Min. funding target§ | 97 | < | 11.88 | 11.92 | 0.74 | 8.70 | 13 |
| K3 | Max. funding target§ | 97 | > | 13.03 | 12.97 | 0.76 | 11.51 | 16 |
| K3 | COVID period | 97 | NA | 0.12 | 0.00 | 0.33 | 0.00 | 1 |
| | Observations | 97 | | | | | | |

as anticipated previously in the definition of our Y1, Y2, Y3, Y4 and Y5 variables. Moreover, even the choice of our independent variables is definitively data-driven, starting from the assumption that they could be

**Table 6.15** Summary statistics Opstart—Italy

| | | *Obs* | t-*test* | *Mean* | *Median* | *Std.Dev* | *Min* | *Max* |
|---|---|---|---|---|---|---|---|---|
| Y1 | Campaign success | 80 | > | 0.85 | 1.00 | 0.36 | 0.00 | 1 |
| Y2/K4 | Percentage raised | 80 | > | 4.93 | 1.51 | 21.87 | 0.02 | 195 |
| Y3/K4 | Capital raised§ | 80 | ≈ | 11.69 | 11.75 | 1.24 | 8.01 | 16 |
| K1 | Entrepreneur gender | 80 | < | 0.07 | 0.00 | 0.27 | 0.00 | 1 |
| K1 | Social media presence | 80 | ≈ | 0.54 | 1.00 | 0.50 | 0.00 | 1 |
| K1 | Social media count | 80 | ≈ | 0.63 | 1.00 | 0.66 | 0.00 | 3 |
| K2 | Pre-money§ | 80 | < | 13.87 | 13.95 | 1.15 | 9.21 | 16 |
| K3 | Share price§ | 80 | > | 6.11 | 5.53 | 1.40 | 4.62 | 12 |
| K3 | Min. funding target§ | 80 | < | 11.21 | 11.23 | 0.99 | 6.22 | 14 |
| K3 | Max. funding target§ | 80 | < | 12.37 | 12.22 | 0.96 | 10.31 | 16 |
| K3 | Max. retail investment§ | 79 | NA | 12.32 | 12.17 | 0.97 | 10.26 | 16 |
| K3 | COVID period | 80 | NA | 0.21 | 0.00 | 0.41 | 0.00 | 1 |
| | Observations | 80 | | | | | | |

obtained from the public information available in ECF platforms. From the previous sections describing data collected in the mining process, we understand that this public information, in a part cannot be used in econometric estimations due to its nature and, consequently, it has been discarded (Data typology A of Fig. 5.1); in another part it is adequate for econometric models and, on the one hand, already studied by literature (Data typology B of Fig. 5.1) and, on the other hand, not studied yet (Data typology C of Fig. 5.1). Besides, effective inclusion of variables in estimations has been conducted after passing multicollinearity tests (i.e., pairwise correlations and Variance Inflation Factor tests) in line with accepted statistical literature.[4]

The following three tables report results of estimates for the three geographical area/country emerging from the platforms selected for this study (see Tables 6.16, 6.17, and 6.18). Each cell indicates if the relationship is statically significant (*$p < 0.10$, **$p < 0.05$, ***$p < 0.010$) and if it is so, the sign and value of the parameter. The room of the cell is grey if the relationship is not statically significant or left blank if the relationship

[4] We followed a common rule of thumb and excluded variables that exceeded the correlation threshold of 0.8 from the models, in line with Belinda and Peat (2014), Young (2017), and Shrestha (2020).

has not been estimated, due to reasons of multicollinearity,[5] or it is not applicable.[6]

Note that in estimating models on dataset obtained merging two, or more, platforms another computational issue arises: estimates exploit the data considering only the variables effectively common among the platforms included in the merge. This implies a reduction of operative data available and explains why, as an example (see Table 6.16), when running models on the geographical area of Anglo-Saxon platforms, we have 14 independent variables, even if Crowdcube could rely on 16 independent variables. Even more importantly, in merging platforms, the number of observations collapses, from the levels of observations in each platform individually considered (e.g., the case of Seedrs with more than 700 observations, and Table 6.16 for the whole Anglo-Saxon area with either 217 or 296 observations). Thus, for the sake of maximizing value of results, we show a selection of dependent variables (Y1, Y2, Y3-Model 3.b or 3.c- and Y4). Moreover, inevitable deduction is that some results might change, based on the geographical width considered. Coherently, we comment if our evidence is a confirmation of, or contrast to, our hypotheses, when possible.

Specifically, in the case of Anglo-Saxon platforms we offer alternative specifications which include (Models A) or exclude (Models B) the independent variable 'Interested investors' which is present only in Crowdcude. This explains why observations fall from 296 observations of Models B to 217 observations of Models A, mainly representing results attributable to Crowdcude indeed.

Regarding results related to the Anglo-Saxon platforms, we note that these platforms tend to disseminate information regarding the human capital of the entrepreneur, while this data is rarely obtainable in the remaining platforms as public information. Nevertheless, in our estimations the variables indicating the entrepreneurial experience end up appearing not-significant, contrary to H1.c which is supposing a positive relationship. The same happens for the age of the entrepreneur, contrary to H1.a, when considering this whole geographical area. Conversely, the

[5] This explains why eventually some variables with enough data to be reported in summary statistics of previous section, do not appear here as regressor in estimations.

[6] The reason might lie in the model specification: in some cases it might correspond to the dependent variable or to a different transformation of it, whether in some other cases it might correspond to a different transformation of an independent variable.

**Table 6.16** Multivariate analysis of Anglo-Saxon platforms

| | Y1 Campaign success (Mod 1) Logit | | Y2 Percentage raised (Mod 2) Linear-log regression | | Y3 Capital raised§ (Mod 3.c) | | Y4 Number of investors (Mod 4) Linear-log regression | |
|---|---|---|---|---|---|---|---|---|
| | (Model A) | (Model B) | (Model A) | (Model B) | (Model A) | (Model B) | (Model A) | (Model B) |
| Entrepreneur age | | | | | | | | |
| Entrepreneur gender | | −0.920* | | | | | | |
| Entrepreneur experience | | | | | | | | |
| Equity retention | | | −0.024*** | −0.041*** | | | | |
| Social media count | | | 0.144* | | | | 140.707* | |
| Pre-money§ | −1.574*** | −1.117** | 0.193*** | 0.284*** | | | | 350.674*** |
| Firm location | | | | | −0.070* | | | 204.437* |
| Firm maturity | | | | | | | | |
| Min. funding target§ | −7.423*** | −6.027*** | −2.296*** | −1.587*** | 0.944*** | 0.939*** | | |
| COVID period | | | | | | | | |
| Interested investors | | | | | 0.00006** | | 0.687*** | |
| Percentage raised | | | | | 0.329*** | 0.432*** | 69.669** | 259.401*** |
| Capital raised§ | 9.461*** | 7.587*** | 2.035*** | 1.168*** | | | | |
| Number of investors | | | 0.0001* | 0.0003*** | | | | |
| *N* | 217 | 296 | 217 | 296 | 217 | 296 | 217 | 298 |

gender variable negatively influences the success of the ECF campaign, meaning that when the project comes from a female entrepreneur, it is less likely to obtain the target capital, practically in line with H1.b which allows alternative expectations. The location of the project within the same geographical area of the platform, in the Anglo-Saxon countries seems to attract a higher number of investors, as the 'Firm location' variable is positively related to the Y4 dependent variables giving evidence of presence of a sort of home country bias, in accordance with H6. Nevertheless, in the truth, the location of the business is negatively related to the Y3 dimension of ECF success, meaning that projects located outside the Anglo-Saxon area tend to raise higher funding.

Interestingly, recall that for the 'Pre-money' variable H5 admits alternative expectations, being either a business evaluation, so affecting positively the odds of success, or an indicator of dimension of the project, with negative expectations. In our estimates it prevails that role of 'Pre-money' as proxy for dimension of the project, involving an inferior likelihood to obtain a success, in terms of mere reaching of the financial goal of the campaign (Y1), even if this implies an increase in the percentage raise (Y2) and an engagement of a larger number of investors (Y4). The same comment is for the significant, but negative relationship of the 'Min. funding target' with relative measures of success (Y1) and (Y2), in accordance with H9, even though involving significant and positive effect in the capital raised (Y3). Interestingly, on the one hand, engagement of the crowd supports the success of the ECF campaigns, indeed. This happens directly with the role of both 'Number of investors', in accordance with H11, and 'Interested investors' on capital raised (in absolute -Y3- and relative -Y2- terms), and indirectly with the positive effect of 'Interested investors' on 'Number of investors'. Nevertheless, information that is very frequently disclosed by platforms, in terms of amount of money already attracted as 'Capital raised', holds a massive positive effect on the success of the campaign for metrics that relate the capital raised in relation to money requested (i.e., the two variables Y1 and Y2). This indicates that the crowd-investors might be induced to participate by the numerosity of the community of investors, for sure. But in the truth they also consider the practical involvement of this crowd, in terms of the money that effectively has been dedicated to the project, in accordance with H10.

Moving to Scandinavian platforms, estimations could rely on a small dataset of overlapping observations/variables, but these few ones are informative as well. In fact, the variable indicating the Social media activity ('Social media count') positively influence the outcome of the ECF campaign, in line with what revealed for Anglo-Saxon platforms and in accordance with H3, even though involving different measures of success. The 'Equity retention' variable here suffers from problem of multicollinearity in the first two models, while when it is applicable it shows a negative relationship with Capital raised (Model 3.b of Table 6.17), partially in line with H2 which admits alternative expectations. Remarkable is that this relationship is comparable to results shown both for Anglo-Saxon and Italian platforms, with a similar statistical significance and sign, even if for different measures of success. A confirmation is offered, also for Scandinavian platforms, in terms of positive effect of the 'Capital raised' variable on the relative measure of success (Y1 and Y2) in accordance with H10, while the home bias for Scandinavian projects here brings about an increase in the percentual capital raised (Y2), in line with H6.

Lastly, merging data of the three Italian platform in Table 6.18, we can confirm comparable results of most of the variables which are common with the other geographical areas (e.g., for Equity retention, Pre-money, Min. funding target, in accordance with H2, H5 and H9, respectively). Conversely, differently from the Anglo-Saxon and the Scandinavian platforms, here the 'Capital raised' variable results not-significant, contrasting with H10. The expected relationship is much more mediated if we want to consider the role of the 'Percentage raised' on the 'Number of investors', within an indirect positive loop between these two variables. Instead, a very relevant difference emerges for Italian platforms when exploiting of the variable 'Professional investors presence', uniquely

**Table 6.17** Multivariate analysis of Scandinavian platforms

| | Y1 Campaign success (Mod 1) Logit | Y2 Percentage raised (Mod 2) Linear-log regression | Y3 Capital raised§ (Mod 3.b) |
|---|---|---|---|
| Social media count | | | 0.265* |
| Equity retention | | | −0.038*** |
| Firm location | | 0.600* | |
| COVID period | −1.047* | | |
| Capital raised§ | 0.853*** | 0.468*** | |
| *N* | 176 | 140 | 185 |

present in 200Crowd and Mamacrowd. As expected, the presence of professional investors is essential for the campaign success, in relative terms and in line with H12. Notably, in Italian platforms, this is the unique variable that explains the Y1 variable, and concurs, with a relevant coefficient, with others for Y2. We anticipate here that no one of the variables used in this study, coming -by definition- from public information, can explain the presence of professional investors. For this reason, we do not include in Table 6.18 the fifth expected dependent variable (Y5).

Note that the dummy variable 'COVID period' is the same consistent control for the period when the campaign was active, and it definitively followed the same rule of computation, given the pandemic was synchronous for the three geographical area considered. Nevertheless, this variable turns out to hold various effects, resulting in a not-significant effect in the Anglo-Saxon area, a negative effect for the Scandinavian platforms (on Y1) and positive effect for Italian platforms (on Y2).

### *6.3.2 Platform-Level Analysis*

We show results of estimations for platforms individually considered, with the awareness that we can rely on a larger number of both variables and observations, because data is not forced to drop for not belonging to the least common denominator of the geographical area/country considered. Inevitable deduction is that some relationship shown in estimations within the comprehensive geographical area here could change, when considering each platform separately. Confirmation of hypotheses may change coherently.

In the following Tables (from Tables 6.19 to 6.28) each cell indicates the sign and value of the parameter when the relationship is statically significant ($^*p < 0.10$, $^{**}p < 0.05$, $^{***}p < 0.010$), whereas the room of the cell is grey when the relationship is not statically significant, or left blank if the relationship has not been estimated, mainly due to reasons of multicollinearity.[7]

[7] For Crowdfunder, Crowdcube, Seedrs, Fundedbyme and Opstart, the 'Social media presence' has been excluded for collinearity with 'Social media count'. The opposite happens in Invesdor and Fundedbyme. Exclusion for multicollinearity has been applied for Capital raised§ in Fundedbyme and Opstart; Firm location in Seedrs, Sowefund and

**Table 6.18** Multivariate analysis of Italian platforms

| | Y1 Campaign success (Mod 1) Logit success | Y2 Percentage raised (Mod 2) Linear-log regression | Y3 Capital raised§ (Mod 3.c) | Y4 Number of investors (Mod 4) Linear-log regression |
|---|---|---|---|---|
| Equity retention | | | −0.085*** | |
| Pre-money§ | | | 0.807** | |
| Min. funding target§ | | −0.747*** | 1.356** | |
| Max. funding target§ | | 0.597*** | | 80.373*** |
| COVID period | | 0.475* | | |
| Percentage raised | | | | 53.141*** |
| Capital raised§ | | | | |
| Number of investors | | 0.003*** | | |
| Professional investors presence | 0.892*** | 1.662*** | | |
| *N* | 145 | 145 | 145 | 145 |

**Table 6.19** Multivariate analysis Crowdfunder—US

| | | Y1 Campaign success | Y2 Percentage raised | Y3 Capital raised | | |
|---|---|---|---|---|---|---|
| | | (Mod1) | (Mod 2) | (Mod 3.a) | (Mod 3.b) | (Mod 3.c) |
| K1 | Entrepreneur gender | | | | | |
| K1 | Social media count | | | | | |
| K2 | Firm location | −2.080* | −0.728** | | | |
| K3 | Share price | | | | | |
| K3 | Share price§ | −0.534** | | | | |
| K3 | Share price^ | | | | | |
| K3 | Min. funding target | | | 0.0001*** | | |
| K3 | Min. funding target§ | | −0.238*** | | | 1.035*** |
| K3 | COVID period | | | | | |
| K4 | Percentage raised | | | 2031.979*** | 4.761*** | 4.830*** |
| K4 | Percentage raised^ | | | −109.381*** | −0.277*** | −0.281*** |
| K4 | Capital raised§ | 1.472*** | −0.384*** | | | |
| K4 | Capital raised^ | | 0.036*** | | | |

In Crowdfunder platform, few variables emerge as public information on entrepreneur human, financial and social capital (K1) and refer to gender and social media count, none of them resulting significant in estimations (see Table 6.19). The unique variable of venture characteristics (K2) is 'Firm location' showing presence of a host country bias, where projects of countries outside the US appear more likely to obtain the campaign success in terms of Y1 and Y2, against H6. Among the K3 variables of campaign characteristics, the 'Share price' negatively affects the success of the campaign Y1, confirming H8; the 'Min. funding target' works as a benchmark for the difficulty of the campaign, similarly for the whole Anglo-Saxon area: the higher this minimum target, the lower the success in relative terms (Y2), even if in absolute terms the capital raised might be higher (Y3). For the variables used as K4 cluster—i.e., objective expressions of the behaviour of investors—we find a dragging effect for 'Percentage raised' on Y3 and for 'Capital raised' on Y1, even though the latter seem to negatively influence the Y2 variable. Note that in Models 2 and 3, we investigated for the presence of a quadratic relationship between independent and dependent variables, finding supporting evidence (see the squared 'Percentage raised^' and 'Capital raised^').

In Crowdcube platform, the data mining procedure collected numerous variables on entrepreneur human, financial and social capital (K1), even if for 'Entrepreneur experience' (variable detected only for this platform) and 'Social media count', we could not obtain significant relationship on any of the various metrics of ECF success (see Table 6.20). Projects presented by male and elder entrepreneurs (as well as mature business) tend to collect higher funding (Y3), but, instead, 'Equity retention', meaning the financial capital dedicated to the project by the entrepreneur, reduces the percentage of capital raised (Y2). As far as K2 variables, we have confirmed evidence of a home bias on investors, given the positive relationship of 'Firm location' with Y4 'Number of investors', even if projects of countries outside UK tend to raise more capital in terms of Y3. The 'Min. funding target' confirms as being a benchmark for the difficulty of the campaign: the higher this minimum target, the lower the success in relative terms (Y1 or Y2), even if in absolute terms the capital raised might be higher (Y3) and it tends to attract more investors (Y4). The 'Percentage raised' confirms a non-linear relationship with the Y3

Mamacrowd; 'Max. funding target' in Sowefund and 200Crowd, 'Percentage raised' in Opstart.

**Table 6.20** Multivariate analysis Crowdcube—UK

| | | Y1 Campaign success | Y2 Percentage raised | Y3 Capital raised | | | Y4 Number investors |
|---|---|---|---|---|---|---|---|
| | | (Mod 1) | (Mod 2) | (Mod 3.a) | (Mod 3.b) | (Mod 3.c) | (Mod 4) |
| K1 | Entrepreneur age | | | | 0.008*** | | |
| K1 | Entrepreneur gender | | | | −0.161** | | |
| K1 | Entrepreneur experience | | | | | | |
| K1 | Equity retention | | −0.040*** | | | | |
| K1 | Social media count | | | | | | |
| K2 | Pre-money | | | 0.00001*** | | | |
| K2 | Pre-money§ | −1.574*** | 0.271*** | | | | 140.262** |
| K2 | Firm location | | | | −0.149* | | 202.611** |
| K2 | Firm maturity | | | | 0.031* | 0.016* | |
| K3 | Min. funding target | | | 0.001*** | 0.000001*** | | |
| K3 | Min. funding target§ | −7.423*** | −1.551*** | | | 0.939*** | 318.498*** |
| K3 | COVID period | | | | | | |
| K4 | Interested investors | | | | | | |
| K4 | Percentage raised | | | 265.634*** | 0.828*** | 0.953*** | 341.916*** |
| K4 | Percentage raised^ | | | −19.650*** | −0.068*** | −0.072*** | |
| K4 | Capital raised§ | *9.461**** | *1.098**** | | | | |
| K4 | Number of investors | | 0.001*** | 0.162*** | | | |
| K4 | Number of investors^ | | −0.00000003** | 0.00002*** | | | |

variable, and, interestingly, it positively affects the number of investors (Y4) showing a herding behaviour of the crowd, as it is going to be discussed in the following section. Even more remarkably, the variable 'Capital raised§', even if positively affecting the success of the campaign as Y1 variable, similar to evidence of Crowdfunder, here, differently to the previous US platform it is also positively (and not negatively) related to the Y2 variable. Lastly, note that the 'Number of investors', used as a K4 independent variable, holds a positive and not linear relationship with the percentage of capital raised (Y2) (Table 6.21).

For the UK Seedrs, the 'Equity retention' variable, differently from previous platforms, shows a positive effect on the percentage of capital raised (Y2), even though a negative non-linear relation with Y3 is noticeable as well. Evidence for the 'Min. funding target' variable is in line with the other Anglo-Saxon countries, while for 'Percentage raised' and 'Capital raised§' evidence is common to those of the UK Crowdcube. Marginally, instead, the 'Share price' positively affects the Y3, contrasting with H8 (Table 6.22).

A short comment for the French Sowefund platform, offering few public information, allows us to collect data on the campaign success (Y1) and a very small number of independent variables. Note that the 'Equity retention' variable, differently from Crowdcube but similarly to Seedrs, shows a positive effect on the relative measure of success, such as here Y1 (Table 6.23).

A brief comment goes, also, to the German Companisto, offering very few data. Note that the Share price, here systematically disclosed, works as a budget constraint, showing a negative relationship with the 'Number of investors' Y4, in contrast with H8, but positively affecting the capital raised Y3, in accordance with H8, with a non-linear relationship. A quadratic relationship also links, in a virtuous loop, the 'Number of investors', as K4, and Capital Raised Y3, in its various forms (Table 6.24).

Few data can be used for estimation of the Swedish Fundedbyme. We note the negative relationship of 'Equity retention' with the Capital raised Y3, similarly to what emerged for Anglo-Saxon area, as well as a significant and positive relationship of the 'Social media presence' to this absolute measure of success (Table 6.25).

Regarding the Finnish Invesdor, we find that projects of female entrepreneurs tend to raise more funding (Y3) but with lower success

**Table 6.21** Multivariate analysis Seedrs—UK

| | | Y1 Campaign success | Y2 Percentage raised | Y3 Capital raised | | | Y4 Number investors |
|---|---|---|---|---|---|---|---|
| | | (Modl) | (Mod 2) | (Mod 3.a) | (Mod 3.b) | (Mod 3.c) | (Mod 4) |
| K1 | Equity retention | | 0.013** | | | −0.382** | |
| K1 | Equity retention^ | | | | | 0.002** | |
| K1 | Social media count | 1.148* | | | −0.234** | 0.147** | 106.6773** |
| K3 | Share price | | | | | | |
| K3 | Share price§ | | | | | 0.070** | |
| K3 | Min funding target Seedrs | | | 0.002*** | 0.000001*** | | |
| K3 | Min funding target§ | −0.921* | −0.320*** | | | 0.936*** | 176.552*** |
| K3 | COVID period | | | | | | |
| K4 | Percentage raised | | | 877.694*** | 0.458*** | 0.398*** | |
| K4 | Capital raised§ | | 0.340*** | | | | |

**Table 6.22** Multivariate analysis Sowefund—France

| | | Y1 Campaign success (Modl) |
|---|---|---|
| K3 | Share price§ | |
| K3 | Min. funding target§ | 0.829** |
| K3 | COVID period | |

in terms of percentage of capital raised (Y2). Anyway, digital social presence positively affect capital raised (Y3) in accordance with H3, as well as yearly positive forecasts, in line with H4. Interestingly, here the home bias is clear, in accordance with H6, with Finnish projects related to higher percentage of capital raised (Y2), compared to foreign projects. Again, here the 'Min. funding target', as already revealed in other platforms, is a level of financial severity of projects, bringing about higher capital raised (Y3) even if percentage of capital raised (Y2) are lower. A confirmation is offered also from the positive and non-linear effect of Percentage raised (K4) on Capital raised (Y3), and the positive effect of 'Capital raised' (K4) on both Campaign success (Y1) and Percentage raised (Y2) (Table 6.26).

Moving towards Italian platforms, we consider 200Crowd and underline two new pieces of evidence, compared to other relationships already known and commented for previous platforms. Firstly, we have the information of presence of Professional investors, both as independent variable (K4) and dependent variable (Y5). In this platform, this presence positively affect the Capital raised (Y3) but it is not significant for the remaining measures of ECF success. Remarkable is that, when presence of Professional investors is used as dependent variable Y5, none of the variables we computed from public information results significant. This is to say that public information regarding the entrepreneur, the venture or the campaign, is not able to explain the presence (or absence) of professional investors. Secondly, we note the effect of the variable 'Interested investors', on the one hand slightly negatively affect the Y2 variable, but on the other hand it positively affects the Number of Investors, that in turn positively affect the same Y2 variable. This is to deduce an effect of the 'Interested investors' variables on ECF campaign that is indirect, on both Y1 and Y2, via the effect of Number of investors (Table 6.27).

For the Mamacrowd platform, we focus on results that could appear distinct, compared to the previous platforms. Firstly, we need to remark that we cannot estimate the logit model (Y1), as a binary measure of

**Table 6.23** Multivariate analysis Companisto—Germany

| | | Y3 Capital raised | | | Y4 Number investors |
|---|---|---|---|---|---|
| | | (Mod3.a) | (Mod3.b) | (Mod3.c) | (Mod4) |
| K3 | Share price | 0.701*** | 0.002*** | | −0.957*** |
| K3 | Share price§ | | | 0.793** | |
| K3 | Share price^ | 0.00004** | −0.0000003*** | | 0.0001*** |
| K3 | COVID period | | | | |
| K4 | Capital raised(t) | | | | 1.456*** |
| K4 | Capital raised(t)^ | | | | −0.0002*** |
| K4 | Number of investors | | 0.004*** | 0.003*** | |
| K4 | Number of investors^ | 0.0003*** | −0.000001*** | −0.000001*** | |

**Table 6.24** Multivariate analysis Fundedbyme—Sweden

| | | Y3 Capital raised | |
|---|---|---|---|
| | | (Mod3.a) | (Mod3.b) |
| K1 | Equity retention | −11.568*** | −0.036*** |
| K1 | Social media presence | 105.266* | 0.522*** |
| K2 | Firm location | | |
| K3 | COVID period | | |

**Table 6.25** Multivariate analysis Invesdor—Finland

| | | | | Y3 Capital raised | | |
|---|---|---|---|---|---|---|
| | | (Mod 1) | (Mod 2) | (Mod 3.a) | (Mod 3.b) | (Mod 3.c) |
| K1 | Entrepreneur gender | | −0.419* | | 0.237* | 0.199** |
| K1 | Social media presence | | | | 0.227* | |
| K2 | Financial forecast (ys) | | | | + * | |
| K2 | Financial forecast | −0.000001*** | | | | |
| K2 | Financial forecast§ | | | | | |
| K2 | Financial forecast^ | 3.80e-14 ** | | | | |
| K2 | Outstanding shares | | | | | |
| K2 | Outstanding shares§ | | | | | |
| K2 | Firm location | | 0.548* | | | |
| K3 | Min. funding target | | | 0.002*** | 0.000002*** | |
| K3 | Min. funding target§ | | −1.708*** | | | 0.987*** |
| K3 | COVID period | | | −208.722** | | |
| K4 | Percentage raised | | | 447.589*** | 0.822*** | 0.909*** |
| K4 | Percentage raised^ | | | −29.837*** | −0.052*** | −0.065*** |
| K4 | Capital raised§ | 2.504*** | 1.597*** | | | |

success, because for this platform the distribution of the variables is too asymmetric, and the estimation does not converge. This means that observations of success (Y1 = 1) are much more frequent than observations of unsuccess (Y1 = 0). Moreover, as for the 200Crowd platform, we did not find any variable obtained from public information able to significantly explain the presence or absence of professional investors (Table 6.28).

The latter, anyway, significantly and positively affect the success of the campaign in terms of percentage of capital raised (Y2). Lastly, we need to pinpoint the uncommon effect of the social media presence of ECF success. If, on the one hand, the numerosity of social media positively affects the number of investors in a campaign (Y4), on the other hand,

**Table 6.26** Multivariate analysis 200Crowd—Italy

| | | Y1 Campaign success | Y2 Percentage raised | Y3 Capital raised | | | Y4 Number investors | Y5 Professional investors |
|---|---|---|---|---|---|---|---|---|
| | | (Mod 1) | (Mod 2) | (Mod 3.a) | (Mod 3.b) | (Mod 3.c) | (Mod 4) | (Mod 5) |
| K1 | Equity retention | | −0.064*** | | | | 1.631* | |
| K2 | Pre-money | | | | | | | |
| K2 | Pre-money§ | | 0.539*** | | | | | |
| K3 | Min. funding target | | | 0.001*** | 0.0002*** | | | |
| K3 | Min. funding target§ | | −1.036*** | | | 1.094*** | 21.091* | |
| K3 | COVID period | | | | | | | |
| K4 | Interested investors | | −0.008* | | | | 1.376*** | |
| K4 | Percentage raised | | | 154.399*** | 0.561*** | 0.636*** | 22.490*** | |
| K4 | Capital raised§ | | 0.422*** | | | | | |
| K4 | Number of investors | 0.558* | 0.013*** | | | | | |
| K4 | Number of investors^ | | −0.00001* | 0.001* | −0.00001** | | | |
| K4 | Professional investors | | | | 1.177*** | 1.133*** | | |

Table 6.27 Multivariate analysis Mamacrowd—Italy

| | | Y2 Percentage raised | Y3 Capital raised | | | Y4 Number of investors | Y5 Professional investorss |
|---|---|---|---|---|---|---|---|
| | | (Mod 2) | (Mod 3.a) | (Mod 3.b) | (Mod 3.c) | (Mod 4) | (Mod 5) |
| K1 | Entrepreneur gender | | | | | | |
| K1 | Equity retention | | | | | | |
| K1 | Social media presence | | −405.319*** | −3.159** | −2.348* | | |
| K1 | Social media count | | | −1.041** | −0.960** | 71.804*** | |
| K2 | Equity | | −0.0001** | −0.000001** | | | |
| K2 | Equity§ | | | | | | |
| K2 | Pre-money | | | 0.0000002* | | | |
| K2 | Pre-money§ | | | | | −220.407* | |
| K2 | Pre-money^ | | | | | 9.712* | |
| K3 | Share price | | | | | | |
| K3 | Share price§ | 0.368** | | | | | |
| K3 | Share price^ | | | | | | |
| K3 | Min. funding target | | | | | | |
| K3 | Min. funding target§ | −0.684*** | | | | | |
| K3 | Max. funding target | | | | | | |
| K3 | Max. funding target§ | 11.955*** | | | 1.313** | −2113.954*** | |
| K3 | Max. funding target^ | −0.447*** | | | | 81.131*** | |
| K3 | COVID period | | 155.293* | 1.657* | | | |
| K4 | Percentage raised | | | | | 57.2*** | |
| K4 | Capital raised§ | | | | | | |
| K4 | Number of investors | 0.014*** | 2.656*** | 0.013** | | | |
| K4 | Number of investors^ | −0.00001*** | −0.001*** | −0.00001* | | | |
| K4 | Professional investors | 0.763** | | | | | |

**Table 6.28** Multivariate analysis Opstart—Italy

| | | Y1 Campaign success | Y3 Capital raised | | |
|---|---|---|---|---|---|
| | | (Mod 1) | (Mod 3.a) | (Mod 3.b) | (Mod 3.c) |
| K1 | Entrepreneur gender | | | | |
| K1 | Social media count | | | | |
| K2 | Pre-money | | | 0.0000001* | |
| K2 | Pre-money§ | | | | |
| K3 | Share price | | 0.015* | | |
| K3 | Share price§ | | | | 0.215** |
| K3 | Min. funding target | | | | |
| K3 | Min. funding target§ | | | | |
| K3 | Min. funding target^ | | | | |
| K3 | Max. funding target | | | −0.00001** | |
| K3 | Max. funding target§ | −2.469* | | | −11.733* |
| K3 | Max. retail investment | | | 0.00001** | |
| K3 | Max retail investment§ | | | | 12.121* |
| K3 | COVID period | −1.632** | | −0.520* | −0.586* |

both the presence in social media, and their variety, negatively affect the capital raised (Y3).

Finally, for the Opstart platform the few public information does not allow to identify particularly relevant relationship, except for the COVID period variable. In fact, this dummy variable has been introduced to indicate projects broadcasted after the pandemic and in most of the cases, until this platform, it resulted not-significant. For Opstart, this variable turns to be significant in three out of four estimates, with a negative sign, indicating that the situation of the pandemic, ceteris paribus, is related to a negative performance of ECF campaigns.

## 6.4 Discussion of Findings

Our discussion is going to deal with these two issues: firstly, the question of presence (or absence) of isomorphism among the 10 ECF platforms analysed; secondly, the emerging investors' preferences in financing new ventures through ECF.

### 6.4.1 *Isomorphism Among ECF Platforms*

The empirical approach of our data mining procedure investigates, initially, *if there is isomorphism in ECF platforms*. Data collected offer three pieces of evidence *against* the presence of such isomorphism (i.e., institutional isomorphism; DiMaggio & Powell, 1983).

#### 6.4.1.1 *First Piece of Evidence: Typologies of Public Information*

Table 6.1 sketches the cross-platforms comparison of the specific public information disclosed, organized in five typologies (on the one hand, the dependent variable Y and, on the other, the four clusters of explanatory variables, from K1 to K4), after cleaning of various information that is too narrow to be analysed (see Subsection 4.3). This allows to observe a radar graph for each platform, where the five axes are representing the Y and the K1, K2, K3 and K4 variables. The length of the blue colour in each axis corresponds to the effective data available for that platform, where the numerosity of variables has been normalized considering all the admissible variables for that typology. This way we obtained very different shapes of radar graphs, with different length of axes based on the different information effectively disclosed by each platform.

As regards the metrics of the dependent variable, we have two platforms that disclose public information that allows the calculation of only one expression of the dependent variable (the French Sowefund, for Y1 and the Swedish FundedByMe, for Y3), a condition that implies that we also have few variables usable as an expression of investor behaviour (K4).

As regards independent variables, the typology in which public information is found concerns less the cluster K2, i.e., the characteristics of the venture for which funding is requested. We are aware that some of the information describing the business was in a format that this research could not handle. In fact, sometimes this information is a qualitative description (text string) of the business, in relation to a sector that is rarely disclosed, or traced back to national classification criteria that would have made the information unusable in an international comparison. Moreover, in many cases the same sectorial classification of the businesses presented for funding requests is reductive and inadequate, since the ECF campaigns are frequently related to innovative projects that are not easily attributable to sectorial predefined categories. In many other cases, then, the information about the venture is contained in a pitch-video that this research has not examined. Therefore, in effect, structured information on the nature of the venture, which can be used in a comparative way in econometric estimates, appears to be the scarcest, being limiter to firm's location. Besides, even the information that should be disseminated on the entrepreneur's human, financial and social capital, K2, appears to have minimal content. For example, objective data on the entrepreneur's experience is disclosed as public information only by one platform (Crowdcube, even though indirectly, through a link to the Companies House's website); socio-demographic data (age and gender) are also scarce. Instead, information relating to the K3 campaign is quite frequent, also due to its nature. Moreover, regarding the technical details of the capital requested, such as the minimum target of funds, results of our estimations appear to be among the most converging within the various platforms considered. Instead, it appears rather surprising that the marker of the starting period of the ECF campaign (pre- or post-pandemic, with the dummy variable 'COVID period') brings out significant differences between countries/geographical areas, as it is going to be discussed in the following.

###### 6.4.1.2 *Second Piece of Evidence: Trade-Off Between Breadth and Depth of Data*

As a declared methodology of this research, we set a list of K4 groups of dependent variables and five different measures for the dependent variable (Y), homogeneous by platforms, most of them already studies by literature. We need to admit that nature of public data collected thanks to the data mining approach prevented us to carry out a unique estimation for all the ten platforms. We uncover a trade-off between breadth of platforms/countries considered and depth of the explanatory variables usable: the wider the geographic area we wish to analyse, the fewer variables and observations available to make the estimates. Therefore, in this research we have given up on carrying out a single estimate on the entire dataset of the data collected. Conversely, we prefer to limit observation of commonalities for similar geographical/cultural areas: Anglo-Saxon platforms/countries, which implicitly also compares non-EU countries with EU countries (one group being the negative of the other group, in our sample of platforms). Within the area of the EU countries, we looked for affinities in the Scandinavian and Italian area, having to give up using the data of the French and German platforms because they were too small. When comparing Anglo-Saxon, Scandinavian and Italian platforms, we have noticed the emergence of some commonalities, for some (e.g., equity retention) but not for all the surviving variables. Consequently, to make the most of the entire database collected, we had to narrow the size of the geographical area down to the detail of the single platform. But this caused that various regularities failed, and the heterogeneities were accentuated, not only in terms of statistical significance but also of sign of the relationship between ECF success and explanatory variables.

#### *6.4.1.3 Third Piece of Evidence: Heterogeneous Projects Screening Procedures*

We can hypothesize a form of isomorphism when ECF platforms, working similarly to financial intermediaries, act selecting projects to disclose in their website. The dominant literature (Kleinert et al., 2022; Löher, 2017) believes that ECF platforms bear a high reputational risk when, based on the pre-screening that they conventionally implement on applications for admission to their website, they accept ECF campaigns with an uncertain outcome. Therefore, it would be reasonable to expect that the success/failure frequency distributions are very similar between platforms because each would like to avoid incurring this reputational risk, operating a reasonably rigorous screening of the campaigns collected on their sites.

To deduce elements in favour of, or against, the existence of this homologation, we carefully observe the expression of success of the ECF campaign in its binary form (Y1, the campaign is successful: yes or no).

The more symmetrical the distributions are, the higher the probability of both success and failure of the ECF campaigns; therefore platforms, on the one hand, assume the reputational/entrepreneurial risk associated with deciding to accept certain campaigns, and on the other hand, they transfer the risk of successful conclusion of the campaign to investors, who may find themselves faced with projects that in the end of the operation do not reach the target of the requested funding. Instead, if the distributions of this binary variable are asymmetric, it can be deduced that the ECF platforms, in their screening, have already banned the projects which, based on their professional experience, most likely will not reach the target, leaving only the projects which are likely to end with the success.

Everything considered, from the data collected in this research, even this form of isomorphism associated with the campaign selection mechanisms is excluded, because our evidence shows how some platforms have implemented a radical selection of the projects to be presented (strongly asymmetric Y1 distributions); other platforms, on the other hand, have also welcomed projects whose success could be more uncertain (more symmetrical distributions of Y1). Among the 10 platforms, for two of these the information on Y1 was not objectively inferable from the public information disclosed. However, of the 8 platforms for which the data was available and usable, the distributions of the binary variable Y1 are characterized by a very different degree of symmetry. The maximally asymmetrical distribution is associated with the campaigns present on the Italian Mamacrowd platform, where the frequency of successes was so high, compared to failures, that it was necessary to abandon the estimate of the logistic model due to the absence of convergence. This confirms that even from the point of view of the strategies and operational mechanisms for project screening, there is no evidence of isomorphism, both within the examined platforms of different geographical areas, and even within the platforms of the same country. In fact, for the other two Italian platforms 200Crowd and Opstart, there is no excessive asymmetry of Y1, as is the case for Mamacrowd, and the logistic estimates have easily converged.

#### *6.4.1.4 Fourth Piece of Evidence: Heterogeneous Presence of Professional Investors*

The presence of institutional investors is explicitly highlighted only for the Italian market, in two platforms directly (Mamacrowd and 200Crowd) and in one platform—Opstart—indirectly, since the data of the 'Max. retail investment' is expected. This evidence is in support of a further proof *against* the presence of isomorphism because two alternatives are possible for non-Italian platforms: (1) either the intervention of professional investors is not envisaged; (2) or professional investors can intervene supporting finance to ECF campaign, but this information is not disseminated as public information.

Obviously, professional investors presence brings inevitable consequences in terms of success of the campaign, resulting in financial resources raise (either in absolute or in relative terms). Moreover, we can note that the evidence of herding behaviour by retail investors does not seem to be supported, given that the presence of professional investors does not seem to affect the overall number of investors attracted by the ECF campaign.

In conclusion, to summarize the role of professional investors, it seems clear that they help to raise capital, and, surprisingly, they do not seem to be imitated by retail investors in our setting. However, using only public information, when we try to understand what drives them to be present, or not, in an ECF campaign, none of the variables used in the research are significant. This leads to the conclusion, as it was quite reasonable to expect, that professional investors are guided using private information, indeed.

### 6.4.2 *Investors' Preferences in Financing New Ventures Through Equity Crowdfunding*

The denial of evidence of isomorphic behaviour of the various ECF platforms observed, implies that it is reasonable to acknowledge that some commonalities can be attributed to the behaviour of investors. For this reason, it is reasonable to research whether there are any correspondences or specificities in the choices to invest in ECF projects.

So now we consider the explanatory variables employed in this research, noting that there are both differences—between platforms—in their relationships with the dimensions of the success of the ECF campaign, and differences, with respect to the existing literature. Nevertheless, the same literature often presents contradictory findings, which can sometimes be explained by reasons attributable to the research approach itself. Different results, in the various papers, can be explained: (i) by the diversity of information, either public or private or a mix, that researchers were able to exploit; (ii) by diversity of metrics used; (iii) or also by a different specification of the models.

Moreover, differences in evidence—among platforms and literature—can be explained by facts attributable also to the different nature of the businesses, that follow one another, in the different financing campaigns. Therefore, discrepancies may be due to the different nature of the demand for capital (by type of entrepreneur, or type of business). Added to this is the fact that the nature of the supply of capital is also evolving: just think of an availability or wealth effect, which in the various historical phases can induce different behaviours in investors, changing their propensity for risk, willingness to diversify with respect to financial portfolios and so on.

An important note is that the various metrics of success of an ECF campaign hold different nuances in meaning: Y1 and Y2 variables are 'relative' measure of success, because they set the result of the campaign in relation to funds that have been requested. These are effective measures of success of the ECF campaign, indeed. On the contrary, the Y3 variable indicates the amount of capital raised, with no reference to the target. A deduction is that some independent variable might affect positively the amount of money raised, but not necessarily this brings to the success of the campaign in relative terms. The same is true for the other Y4 and Y5 variables (this latter, very marginally, because we found that public information is not able to explain the presence of professional investors). Again, some independent variables might positively influence the number of investors attracted within a campaign, but it is not given for granted that the ECF campaign reaches the Y1 and Y2 level of success. In the cases in which the number of investors has been proven to increase the relative measure of success Y1 and Y2 (but only in this case), we could claim the presence of an indirect effect of that independent variable on the ECF success, mediated via the number of investors.

We now proceed by selecting the most recurring explanatory variables as significant in our estimates, following the order of the four clusters and noting the affinities or differences, both by geographical area and/or platform, and with respect to the existing literature.

As anticipated, for K1 cluster of variables we have few platforms indicating socio-demographic features of the entrepreneur. Only for Crowdcube we have evidence of a relation of age (positive only with Y3) but we do not find similar results in literature because this variable has been studied in relation to the Y1 (Ralcheva & Roosenboom, 2020) for Crowdcube and Seedrs, and in relation to Y2 (Löher et al., 2018), showing a negative sign. In our estimates, gender confirms contradictory sign as shown in preceding literature, in rare case in which it appears significant (negative with Y2 for Investor, negative and positive with Y3 for Crowdcube and Investor, respectively).

Entrepreneur experience, as already underlined, is public information disseminated only for Crowdcube platform and in our estimates its relationship with success appears not-significant, partially not in line with literature, but when referring to Y1 it is in line with Vismara (2019) and Shafi (2021); and with Y3 and Y4, it is in line with Barbi and Mattioli (2019). The first deduction could be that human capital, as specialized skills measured by this variable, appears not to affect the ECF success. But this conclusion needs to be left open because we presume that the specialized human capital has been mis-measured by the variable used, considering all the remaining information ended up into narrative descriptions, as well as the video-pitch, of the venture and of the entrepreneur, that in this research could not be considered.

'Equity retention' reveals one of the most consistent, but also debatable, relationships among our explanatory variables, resulting significantly and negatively related to success, with unique exception of Seedrs, showing a positive link with Y2—but negative with Y3—and 200Crowd showing a positive link with Y4, i.e., the number of investors. We argue that the prevailing negative link of 'Equity retention' with our Y2 and Y3 metrics of success works as a sign of distrust towards the entrepreneur if she has put her own money into it, showing a scepticism towards her over-confidence (Singh, 2020). However, in the Seedrs platform, where the relationship is positive, this happens for the variable Y2 simultaneously showing a negative relationship on Y3, and with a non-linear effect, in line with Coakley et al. (2022). Interestingly, the positive sign of 'Equity retention' on the number of investors (Y4) may confirm the herding effect moving the choice of crowd-investors being influenced by the 'skin-in the-game' they deduce by the amount of money the entrepreneur personally put on the project.

Anyway, all considered, our results appear only partially in line with literature that, in the truth, offers various results, based on different platforms explored and metrics of success. As an example, for the quadratic relationship between 'Equity retention' and success uncovered in our estimates in Seedrs platform we are in line with Coakley et al. (2022) and partially in line with Vismara (2016). Conversely, the link between 'Equity retention' and the Y1 variable is never significant in our dataset, while it appears to be significantly and positively related to Y1 in papers of Cumming et al. (2019), Vismara (2019), Ralcheva and Roosenboom (2020), and Shafi (2021). Instead, for the positive relationship with Y4, our results are in line with Vismara (2016) and Vismara (2019), even if refereeing to different platforms. Lastly, our results are in line in line with Piva and Rossi-Lamastra (2018) for it's not a significant relationship to ECF success in Mamacrowd platform.

As far as the digital social capital of the entrepreneur, measured by the 'Social media presence' or 'Social media count' variables, we know that literature is converging in showing a positive effect on ECF success (among the others, Nitani et al. [2019], Piva and Rossi-Lamastra [2018], Lukkarinen et al. [2016], Vismara [2016]). This evidence is mostly confirmed in our estimates with two exceptions of a negative relationship with the Y3 variable of success, and for Seerds and Mamacrowd platforms. Anyway, for this latter Italian platform, we remark the statistically significant and positive influence of 'Social media count' on Y4, i.e., the Number of investors engaged in the ECF campaign.

As far as the variables included in K3—i.e., features of the venture—we focus on results on the 'Pre-money' variable, with contradictory evidence from literature, mostly platform-specific. In line with literature, in our estimates, the prevailing significant relation of 'Pre-money' is positive with Y2, Y3 and Y4, involving various platforms. Instead, there is a negative relationship of this variable with the Y1 campaign success in Crowdcube; a negative and non-linear relationship has been uncovered with the Y4 Number of investors in Mamacrowd.

Noticeable is that, while the 'Firm location' variable is consistently not-significant, our estimates show that, in Crowdfunder platform, ventures based outside the US reduce their odds for having success in ECF campaigns (negative sign for both Y1 and Y2 variables), and the opposite is true for Invesdor platform. Interestingly, for Crowdcube, ventures based in the UK attract more investors, Y4 (presence of a home bias), even if they reduce capital raised (Y3).

Among the variables included in the K3 cluster, we discuss the results of 'Min. funding target', that existing literature ambiguously related to measure of ECF success, with various evidence very platform-specific and depending on the Y dependent variable. On the contrary, in our estimates, the 'Min. funding target' variable shows the most stable and consistent evidence among the platforms considered. With exception of the French Sowefund, that is very small indeed, we find for all the remaining platform the 'Min. funding target' negatively affects the relative measure of success (Y1 and Y2) but at the same, it is positively related to the amount of capital raised (Y3). Interpretation of this evidence need to recall the complementary information of the relative (Y1 and Y2) and absolute (Y3) measures of success of ECF campaign. Our results easily identify the role of the 'Min. funding target' as a benchmark for the *difficulty* of the campaign, meaning that the higher the target, the less likely it can be reached, even if the effort in terms of money raised is higher.

For K3 cluster, a brief comment goes to various results obtained by the time marker for the pandemic ('COVID period' variable). For quite all the platforms/geographical areas considered, this variable is not significant, meaning that there was no significant chance of the observed relationships before and after the pandemic. Exceptions are the Finnish

Investors and the Italian Opstart with a significant negative sign of this variable, in relation to Y3 for the first platform, and to both Y1 and Y3 for the last one; in this case, evidence indicates a significant contraction of the ECF business with the pandemic. But, on the contrary, the Mamacrowd platform, Italian as well, recorded opposite evidence, with a positive sign of the 'COVID period' variable, *ceteris paribus*, with Y3 measure of success.

Finally, some comments are due on the most relevant relationships uncovered for variables belonging to the K4 cluster. The new variable 'Interested investors', never studied in literature before, appears seldom significant, but when it does (in the 200Crowd platform) it indicates a positive effect on Y4—i.e., Number of Investors engaged by the campaign—even if negatively affects the amount of money raised (Y3). We recall that the 'Percentage raised', has been studied by existing literature as dependent variables, but it appears not studied as independent variable, yet, as we did. After controlling for collinearity issues, interestingly, it shows a quadratic relationship with Y3, in many platforms, and it reveals a positive influence on the number of investors engaged (Y4) for Crowdcube, 200Crowd and Mamacrowd. We argue that this could mean that crowd-investors are influenced by the financial commitment that others demonstrated having put their money on the project. This 'herding drag' could be the same process behind the positive relationship shown on the 'Capital raised' variable.

As far as the general effect of the *numerosity* of the crowd on the success of campaign, where existing literature is consistently converging in expecting a positive effect, our results indicate a situation that appears slightly more complicated. In fact, in our estimates the relationship between Number of investors and success of ECF campaigns, among the ten platforms observed, turns out to be significantly and positively affecting Y1 only for the 200Crowd platform, and affecting Y2, only for three platforms (Crowdcube, 200Crowd and Mamacrowd). In the remaining cases, it is not significant.

## References

Barbi, M., & Mattioli, S. (2019). Human capital, investor trust, and equity crowdfunding. *Research in International Business and Finance, 49*, 1–12.

Belinda, B., & Peat, J. (2014). *Medical statistics: A guide to SPSS, data analysis, and critical appraisal* (2nd ed.). Wiley.

Coakley, J., Lazos, A., & Liñares-Zegarra, J. M. (2022). Equity crowdfunding founder teams: Campaign success and venture failure. *British Journal of Management, 33*(1), 286–305.
Cumming, D., Meoli, M., & Vismara, S. (2019). Investors' choices between cash and voting rights: Evidence from dual-class equity crowdfunding. *Research Policy, 48*(8), 103740.
DiMaggio, P. J., & Powell, W. W. (1983). The iron cage revisited: Institutional isomorphism and collective rationality in organizational fields. *American Sociological Review, 48*(2), 147–160.
Kleinert, S., Bafera, J., Urbig, D., & Volkmann, C. K. (2022). Access denied: How equity crowdfunding platforms use quality signals to select new ventures. *Entrepreneurship Theory and Practice, 46*(6), 1626–1657. https://doi.org/10.1177/10422587211011945
Löher, J. (2017). The interaction of equity crowdfunding platforms and ventures: An analysis of the preselection process. *Venture Capital, 19*(1–2), 51–74.
Löher, J., Schneck, S., & Werner, A. (2018). A research note on entrepreneurs' financial commitment and crowdfunding success. *Venture Capital, 20*(3), 309–322.
Lukkarinen, A., Teich, J. E., Wallenius, H., & Wallenius, J. (2016). Success drivers of online equity crowdfunding campaigns. *Decision Support Systems, 87*, 26–38.
Nitani, M., Riding, A., & He, B. (2019). On equity crowdfunding: Investor rationality and success factors. *Venture Capital, 21*(2–3), 243–272.
Piva, E., & Rossi-Lamastra, C. (2018). Human capital signals and entrepreneurs' success in equity crowdfunding. *Small Business Economics, 51*(3), 667–686.
Ralcheva, A., & Roosenboom, P. (2020). Forecasting success in equity crowdfunding. *Small Business Economics, 55*(1), 39–56.
Shafi, K. (2021). Investors' evaluation criteria in equity crowdfunding. *Small Business Economics, 56*(1), 3–37.
Shrestha, N. (2020). Detecting multicollinearity in regression analysis. *American Journal of Applied Mathematics and Statistics, 8*, 39–42. https://doi.org/10.12691/ajams-8-2-1
Singh, R. P. (2020). Overconfidence: A common psychological attribute of entrepreneurs which leads to firm failure. *New England Journal of Entrepreneurship, 23*(1), 25–39.
Vismara, S. (2016). Equity retention and social network theory in equity crowdfunding. *Small Business Economics, 46*(4), 579–590.
Vismara, S. (2019). Sustainability in equity crowdfunding. *Technological Forecasting and Social Change, 141*, 98–106.
Young, D. S. (2017). *Handbook of regression methods* (pp. 109–136). CRC Press.

CHAPTER 7

# Conclusions and Contributions to Theory and Practice

**Abstract** This section concludes the manuscript and offers an overview of the work, as well as the main contributions to theory and practice.

**Keywords** Equity crowdfunding · Campaign success · Theoretical implications · Policy recommendation

This research innovates economic literature in its methodology based on a data mining procedure that captures public data offered on the Internet by ten different ECF platforms around the world. It followed a *hybrid* data analysis approach, as the pattern of knowledge was not guided by machine learning, as it appears usual in data science literature, but it reconciled, when possible, public data to traditional variables and hypotheses expected from ECF literature. So, this study is unique in terms of comparing the same exploratory setting against evidence shown by campaigns recorded for a large timespan and within a cross-country, cross-platform perspective. The information set available from platforms' websites definitively guides the decision-making of retail investors, but at the same time, may attest evidence of isomorphism in the disclosure strategy of ECF platforms.



F. J. Mazzocchini and C. Lucarelli, *Investors' Preferences in Financing New Ventures*,
https://doi.org/10.1007/978-3-031-30058-5_7

Coherently, analysis of our unique dataset gives answer to two research questions: the first issue is whether there is isomorphism among ECF platforms inferable from publicly available information displayed by ECF platforms. The answer is negative, based on four pieces of evidence: the typologies of public information disclosed are different, both in types (e.g., regarding the feature of entrepreneurs, the ventures, the campaigns or the behaviour of the other investors) and in details offered regarding each type. These differences impose a trade-off between breadth and depth of data analysis, creating practical (numerical) barriers in undertaking a comprehensive cross-country, cross-platform comparison. This reinforces support against *feasibility* of isomorphism in its three possible dimension, both *mimetic* because managers of ECF platforms cannot clearly observe behaviours of their competitors, *coercive*, because regulation of ECF seems to remain quite scattered at the international level and also *professional/normative*, because advisors do not seem sharing their knowledge about what could be the best offer of public information driving the ECF campaign success. This absence of isomorphism is then emphasized by evidence of significant heterogeneity of project screening procedures among managers of ECF platforms when, on the one hand, there is a large number of platforms accepting the risk that an ECF is not going to collect the targeted funding. On the other hand, there are other platforms disclosing projects that will most likely receive the requested money. Finally, the worldwide cross-platform comparison indicates heterogeneous presence of professional investors.

The second question of this research is to understand if crowd-investors, in different countries, tend to follow similar decision-making process, and given that, what are the signals effectively learnt by retail investors, among those made publicly available, leading investors' preferences and thus bring to success of a fundraising campaign. The ECF investing support expectations that unsophisticated crowd-investors could be positively and significantly affected by signals received as public information, as well as they may follow herd behaviours observing the choice of both professionals and the crowd itself. In fact, ECF investors could tend to act as 'birds of a feather flock together', as we may expect that early bird investors have the capability of convincing late and undecided ones.

Nevertheless, the analysis of our dataset, comparing various campaigns recorded for a large timespan and within a cross-country and cross-platform perspective, confirms that the decision-making process of ECF investors is very unlikely to be identical worldwide. In the truth, when we compared existent ECF literature specifying the platforms observed and the metric used for campaign success, we found the presence of quite contradictory findings concerning the drivers of ECF decision-making. So, we were forced to set research hypotheses but being aware that we could find results mostly in favour, but also, occasionally, against them.

In fact, our estimates conclude with an overall view of the drivers that are more systemically relevant, in significance and sign. Nevertheless, this is not granted for sure for each variable/metric/platform considered. In a short and simplified summary of our findings, on the one hand, we have evidence that some features of the entrepreneurs (age, gender and entrepreneur experience), of the venture (firm location) and of the campaign (share price) offer the most contradictory evidence among platforms. On the other hand, we find quite convergent results of other drivers, such as equity retention, pre-money and firm maturity (but with sign not always concordant in extant literature) or minimum funding target and engagement of investors, in terms of money collected and in numbers, both retail and professional.

A simple confirmation of heterogeneity in ECF investors' decision-making is offered by the variable 'COVID period', used as the same consistent control for the period when the campaign was active, given the pandemic was synchronous for the geographical area considered. Remarkably, this variable turns out to be: not significant in the Anglo-Saxon area, negatively related to campaign success for the Scandinavian platforms and positively related for the Italian platforms.

## 7.1 Limitations of the Study

We acknowledge at least four limitations of this research. Firstly, we are aware that there is an amount of public information that we had to discard, such as the description of project/entrepreneur offered in extended text explanations—sometimes disclosing the business sector—or also the description of project/entrepreneur in the audio–video format of pitch videos. We admit that we processed information mainly in numerical format (hard information), and we did not perform text analysis, or video analysis. However, we are aware that soft drivers of decision-making such as *trust*, or *empathy*, could hold a strong impact, especially when considering non-professional investors, as most crowd-investors. So, we are aware that we are neglecting, here, an important amount of (public) information that might be relevant in explaining the success of ECF campaigns.

A second limitation is that here we assume that public information is spontaneous and genuine. In truth, signalling mechanism might also be used for bad practices and induce moral hazard. Indeed, entrepreneurs themselves or platform managers might manipulate this information by making a non-confirmed bid during the campaign and withdraw the investment before the conclusion to attract late investor. Therefore, if retail investors are aware of these bad practices, they could not rely on this source of information alone.

A third weakness of this research is that if, on the one hand, we observe absence of isomorphism among ECF platforms, on the other hand, we did not investigate the possible reasons for such differences, that could be due to various technological barriers, or also to dissimilar regulatory setting, worldwide. Interestingly, having noted that there is also heterogeneity in crowd-investors' behaviour, we cannot exclude that absence of isomorphism is induced by the fact that platform managers differently responded to different (cultural?) need of both investors and entrepreneurs.

Finally, we need to admit that in this research we considered a specific expression of success, in the process of ECF, that is the *success* of the *campaign*. But we are aware that the *success* of the *campaign* is not the *success* of the *venture* (i.e., post-offering success). Our dataset could not respond to the very important question that is whether the money collected during the ECF allowed the further steps of the new firm creation. Similarly, it cannot provide answers to whether the created firm finally resulted in a profitable firm, allowing to conclude that the ECF investment was a good investment for an investor's perspective. Further research in the field could respond to these unsolved questions.

## 7.2 Theoretical and Practical Implications

Negations of isomorphism in disclosure (and operational) strategies of ECF platforms, as well as the confirmation of heterogeneity in the decision-making of crowd-investors, open to further investigation, firstly at the theoretical level. Models of behaviours under risk may integrate conventional variables with new (soft) drivers that effectively influence investors' decisions. ECF investment could be a simplified expression of choice under risk where new theories could be tested with easily accessible data. With this purpose, ECF websites end up being a huge repository of information thanks to the systematic storage of a mass of data, both in the conventional form of hard information (numbers) but also in a non-conventional form (such, text or audio-video). In the virtuous loop that must exist between theory and practice, this availability of unstructured data may inspire creation of innovative theoretical models of decision-making under risk.

As concluding remarks, the COVID-19 pandemic seems to have fostered investments in ECF. Results showed a rise in transactions, and significant impact on the amount of capital raised. This is probably due to the increment of digitalization and FinTech usage during lockdowns imposed by countries where the ECF campaigns were listed, as well as to the resilient adoption of innovative and inclusive marketing and promoting means. This suggests that the ECF market could grow further in the future, as is happening to all the expressions of FinTech, which are making themselves complementary in the functions of traditional financial markets and intermediaries, especially in supporting the financial needs associated with the creation of new businesses. Note also that data has been collected between 2019 and 2020, but lately many ECF platforms have increased the set of information provided. We believe that platforms at the time of this writing are facing an information explosion phase and could move towards institutional isomorphism shortly.

# Appendix: Analytical Results of Estimations

## Country-Level Estimates

See Tables A.1, A.2, and A.3.



F. J. Mazzocchini and C. Lucarelli, *Investors' Preferences in Financing New Ventures*,
https://doi.org/10.1007/978-3-031-30058-5

**Table A.1** Multivariate analysis of Anglo-Saxon platforms

| | *(1a) Campaign success* | *(1b) Campaign success* | *(2a) Percentage raised* | *(2b) Percentage raised* | *(3a) Capital raised§* | *(3b) Capital raised§* | *(4a) Number of investors* | *(4b) Number of investors* |
|---|---|---|---|---|---|---|---|---|
| Entrepreneur age | 0.016 | −0.0002 | −0.003 | −0.002 | 0.001 | 0.002 | −2.061 | −3.979 |
| | (0.04) | (0.02) | (0.004) | (0.003) | (0.001) | (0.002) | (3.86) | (3.67) |
| Entrepreneur gender | −1.253 | −0.920* | −0.078 | −0.118 | −0.021 | −0.027 | 124.366 | 80.237 |
| | (0.81) | (0.55) | (0.09) | (0.09) | (0.04) | (0.05) | (90.17) | (92.59) |
| Entrepreneur experience | −0.214 | −0.117 | 0.005 | 0.013 | 0.004 | −0.002 | −7.534 | 2.283 |
| | (0.40) | (0.21) | (0.02) | (0.02) | (0.01) | (0.01) | (21.03) | (23.42) |
| Equity retention | 0.029 | 0.062 | −0.024*** | −0.041*** | −0.0001 | −0.004 | 13.289 | −11.334 |
| | (0.09) | (0.07) | (0.01) | (0.01) | (0.003) | (0.01) | (8.46) | (9.18) |
| Social media count | 0.161 | 0.266 | 0.144* | 0.111 | −0.031 | 0.062 | 140.707* | 75.893 |
| | (0.83) | (0.56) | (0.08) | (0.08) | (0.03) | (0.05) | (78.30) | (86.22) |
| Pre-money§ | −1.574*** | −1.117** | 0.193*** | 0.284*** | 0.009 | 0.064 | 67.070 | 350.674*** |
| | (0.56) | (0.44) | (0.06) | (0.07) | (0.03) | (0.04) | (45.83) | (42.10) |
| Firm location | −1.153 | 0.113 | 0.077 | 0.021 | −0.070* | −0.078 | 66.074 | 204.437* |
| | (1.92) | (0.76) | (0.10) | (0.10) | (0.04) | (0.06) | (96.39) | (104.01) |
| Firm maturity | 0.271 | 0.174 | 0.0003 | −0.006 | 0.004 | 0.014 | 6.462 | 1.755 |
| | (0.40) | (0.20) | (0.02) | (0.02) | (0.01) | (0.01) | (17.88) | (20.33) |
| Min. funding target§ | −7.423*** | −6.027*** | −2.296*** | −1.587*** | 0.944*** | 0.939*** | | |
| | (1.93) | (1.11) | (0.08) | (0.08) | (0.03) | (0.05) | | |

| | *(1a) Campaign success* | *(1b) Campaign success* | *(2a) Percentage raised* | *(2b) Percentage raised* | *(3a) Capital raised§* | *(3b) Capital raised§* | *(4a) Number of investors* | *(4b) Number of investors* |
|---|---|---|---|---|---|---|---|---|
| COVID period | 0.756 | 0.292 | 0.069 | −0.023 | −0.040 | 0.010 | 135.349 | 154.219 |
| | (1.03) | (0.62) | (0.09) | (0.10) | (0.04) | (0.06) | (92.97) | (99.53) |
| Interested investors | −0.001 | | 0.00002 | | 0.00006** | | 0.687*** | |
| | (0.002) | | (0.00007) | | (0.00002) | | (0.05) | |
| Percentage raised | | | | | 0.329*** | 0.432*** | 69.669** | 259.401*** |
| | | | | | (0.02) | (0.03) | (32.81) | (33.37) |
| Capital raised§ | 9.461*** | 7.587*** | 2.035*** | 1.168*** | | | | |
| | (2.17) | (1.26) | (0.10) | (0.07) | | | | |
| Number of investors | 0.002 | 0.002 | 0.0001* | 0.0003*** | −0.00002 | −9.59e-06 | | |
| | (0.005) | (0.002) | (0.00007) | (0.0001) | (0.00003) | (0.00003) | | |
| Constant | −2.718 | −8.153 | 3.349*** | 5.854*** | 0.345 | −0.377 | −2547.036*** | −4262.870*** |
| | (12.75) | (8.20) | (1.04) | (1.03) | (0.43) | (0.66) | (801.29) | (850.07) |
| *N* | 217 | 296 | 217 | 296 | 217 | 296 | 217 | 298 |
| *R*-squared | | | 0.85 | 0.76 | 0.96 | 0.89 | 0.71 | 0.44 |
| AIC | 82.33 | 135.22 | 350.00 | 582.24 | −45.32 | 287.98 | 3354.41 | 4722.51 |
| BIC | 129.65 | 183.20 | 397.32 | 630.22 | 2.00 | 335.96 | 3394.97 | 4763.18 |

Columns ref to Coef./(Std. err.) $^{*}p < 0.10$, $^{**}p < 0.05$, $^{***}p < 0.010$

**Table A.2** Multivariate analysis of Scandinavian platforms

| | *(1)* *Campaign success* *Coef./(Std. err.)* | *(2)* *Percentage raised* *Coef./(Std. err.)* | *(3b)* *Capital raised§* *Coef./(Std. err.)* |
|---|---|---|---|
| Social media count | −0.343 | −0.354 | 0.265* |
| | (0.57) | (0.22) | (0.14) |
| Firm location | −0.234 | 0.600* | −0.086 |
| | (0.69) | (0.35) | (0.18) |
| COVID period | −1.047* | 0.381 | 0.189 |
| | (0.63) | (0.26) | (0.21) |
| Equity retention | | | −0.038*** |
| | | | (0.01) |
| Capital raised§ | 0.853*** | 0.468*** | |
| | (0.25) | (0.09) | |
| Constant | −7.382*** | −4.477*** | 15.038*** |
| | (2.79) | (1.13) | (0.88) |
| *N* | 176 | 140 | 185 |
| *R*-squared | | 0.21 | 0.09 |
| AIC | 114.32 | 454.31 | 555.49 |
| BIC | 130.18 | 469.02 | 571.59 |

$^{*}p < 0.10$, $^{**}p < 0.05$, $^{***}p < 0.010$

**Table A.3** Multivariate analysis of Italian platforms

| | *(1)*<br>*Campaign success*<br>*Coef./(Std. err.)* | *(2)*<br>*Percentage raised*<br>*Coef./(Std. err.)* | *(3b)*<br>*Capital raised§*<br>*Coef./(Std. err.)* | *(4)*<br>*Number of investors*<br>*Coef./(Std. err.)* |
|---|---|---|---|---|
| Equity retention | 0.0003 | 0.008 | −0.085*** | 1.164 |
| | (0.001) | (0.01) | (0.03) | (1.49) |
| Pre-money§ | 0.010 | 0.018 | 0.807** | 7.616 |
| | (0.02) | (0.11) | (0.33) | (15.53) |
| Min. funding target§ | −0.009 | −0.747*** | 1.356** | 33.700 |
| | (0.03) | (0.20) | (0.65) | (30.43) |
| Max. funding target§ | −0.009 | 0.597*** | −0.299 | 80.373*** |
| | (0.03) | (0.21) | (0.66) | (29.79) |
| COVID period | −0.054 | 0.475* | 0.713 | −42.636 |
| | (0.04) | (0.28) | (0.89) | (41.40) |
| Percentage raised | | | 0.194 | 53.141*** |
| | | | (0.27) | (11.54) |
| Capital raised§ | 0.003 | 0.020 | | 3.463 |
| | (0.004) | (0.03) | | (3.97) |
| Number of investors | 0.000006 | 0.003*** | 0.002 | |
| | (0.00007) | (0.00) | (0.002) | |
| Professional investor | 0.892*** | 1.662*** | 1.336 | −7.388 |
| | (0.04) | (0.26) | (0.93) | (43.45) |
| Constant | 0.118 | 0.289 | −9.317 | −1675.590*** |
| | (0.34) | (2.37) | (7.35) | (311.53) |
| *N* | 145 | 145 | 145 | 145 |
| *R*-squared | 0.83 | 0.49 | 0.21 | 0.39 |
| AIC | −102.96 | 459.98 | 789.61 | 1902.54 |
| BIC | −76.17 | 486.77 | 816.40 | 1929.33 |

$^{*}p < 0.10$, $^{**}p < 0.05$, $^{***}p < 0.010$

## Platform-Level Estimates

See Tables A.4, A.5, A.6, A.7, A.8, A.9, A.10, A.11, A.12, and A.13.

**Table A.4** Multivariate analysis for Crowdfunder.com

| | *(1) Campaign success Coef./(Std. err.)* | *(2) Percentage raised Coef./(Std. err.)* | *(3a) Capital raised (thousands) Coef./(Std. err.)* | *(3b) Capital raised§ Coef./(Std. err.)* | *(3c) Capital raised§ Coef./(Std. err.)* |
|---|---|---|---|---|---|
| Entrepreneur gender | 1.277 | −0.214 | −176.986 | 1.571 | 1.699 |
| | (1.19) | (0.35) | (285.47) | (1.42) | (1.35) |
| Social media count | −0.426 | −0.080 | 205.705 | 0.246 | −0.132 |
| | (0.57) | (0.20) | (156.55) | (0.78) | (0.76) |
| Firm location | −2.080* | −0.728** | 345.237 | 2.038 | 1.675 |
| | (1.11) | (0.30) | (249.39) | (1.24) | (1.15) |
| COVID period | 0.769 | 0.142 | −109.720 | 1.623 | 1.328 |
| | (1.33) | (0.35) | (278.87) | (1.39) | (1.32) |
| Share price | | | −0.010 | 0.00001 | |
| | | | (0.01) | (0.00005) | |
| Share price§ | −0.534** | 0.376 | | | −0.097 |
| | (0.24) | (0.27) | | | (0.24) |
| Share price^ | | −0.026 | | | |
| | | (0.02) | | | |
| Min. funding target | | | 0.0001*** | 2.09e-07 | |
| | | | (0.00003) | (1.44e-07) | |
| Min. funding target§ | | −0.238*** | | | 1.035*** |
| | | (0.09) | | | (0.32) |
| Percentage raised | | | 2031.979*** | 4.761*** | 4.830*** |
| | | | (141.77) | (0.71) | (0.68) |
| Percentage of capital raised^ | | | −109.381*** | −0.277*** | −0.281*** |
| | | | (10.89) | (0.05) | (0.05) |

(continued)

**Table A.4** (continued)

| | *(1)* *Campaign success* *Coef./(Std. err.)* | *(2)* *Percentage raised* *Coef./(Std. err.)* | *(3a)* *Capital raised (thousands)* *Coef./(Std. err.)* | *(3b)* *Capital raised§* *Coef./(Std. err.)* | *(3c)* *Capital raised§* *Coef./(Std. err.)* |
|---|---|---|---|---|---|
| Capital raised§ | 1.472*** | −0.384*** | | | |
| | (0.37) | (0.08) | | | |
| Capital raised^ | | 0.036*** | | | |
| | | (0.01) | | | |
| Constant | −15.023*** | 2.607* | −583.828** | 3.966*** | −8.583* |
| | (4.53) | (1.44) | (230.47) | (1.15) | (4.35) |
| *N* | 129 | 129 | 122 | 122 | 129 |
| *R*-squared | | 0.39 | 0.73 | 0.35 | 0.39 |
| Pseudo $R^2$ | 0.57 | | | | |
| AIC | 58.49 | 435.51 | 2037.09 | 743.84 | 781.80 |
| BIC | 78.50 | 464.10 | 2062.32 | 769.08 | 807.54 |

$^{*}p < 0.10$, $^{**}p < 0.05$, $^{***}p < 0.010$

**Table A.5** Multivariate analysis for Crowdcube

| | *(1) Campaign success* | *(2) Percentage raised* | *(3a) Capital raised (thousands)* | *(3b) Capital raised§* | *(3c) Capital raised§* | *(4) Number of investors* |
|---|---|---|---|---|---|---|
| | *Coef./(S.E.)* | *Coef./(S.E.)* | *Coef./(S.E.)* | *Coef./(S.E.)* | *Coef./(S.E.)* | *Coef./(S.E.)* |
| Entrepreneur experience | −0.214 | 0.013 | 3.085 | −0.013 | −0.003 | −0.912 |
| | (0.40) | (0.02) | (8.62) | (0.02) | (0.01) | (23.02) |
| Entrepreneur age | 0.016 | −0.001 | 0.173 | 0.008*** | −0.001 | −4.897 |
| | (0.04) | (0.003) | (1.34) | (0.002) | (0.001) | (3.62) |
| Entrepreneur gender | −1.253 | −0.121 | 21.306 | −0.161** | −0.008 | 113.132 |
| | (0.81) | (0.09) | (34.05) | (0.07) | (0.04) | (91.46) |
| Equity retention | 0.029 | −0.040*** | 1.902 | −0.006 | 0.001 | 9.440 |
| | (0.09) | (0.01) | (3.32) | (0.01) | (0.00) | (10.59) |
| Social media count | 0.161 | 0.100 | −23.318 | 0.071 | 0.008 | 75.294 |
| | (0.83) | (0.08) | (32.18) | (0.07) | (0.04) | (84.96) |
| Pre-money | | | 6.62e-06*** | 1.32e-09 | | |
| | | | (9.99e-07) | (2.17e-09) | | |
| Pre-money§ | −1.574*** | 0.271*** | | | 0.036 | 140.262** |
| | (0.56) | (0.07) | | | (0.03) | (70.47) |
| Firm location | −1.153 | 0.005 | −62.887 | −0.149* | −0.056 | 202.611** |
| | (1.92) | (0.10) | (38.53) | (0.08) | (0.04) | (102.43) |
| Firm maturity | 0.271 | −0.007 | −2.383 | 0.031* | 0.016* | −3.110 |
| | (0.40) | (0.02) | (7.50) | (0.02) | (0.01) | (20.06) |
| Min. funding target§ | −7.423*** | −1.551*** | | | 0.939*** | 318.498*** |
| | (1.93) | (0.08) | | | (0.03) | (121.20) |

(continued)

**Table A.5** (continued)

| | (1) *Campaign success* | (2) *Percentage raised* | (3a) *Capital raised (thousands)* | (3b) *Capital raised§* | (3c) *Capital raised§* | (4) *Number of investors* |
|---|---|---|---|---|---|---|
| | *Coef./(S.E.)* | *Coef./(S.E.)* | *Coef./(S.E.)* | *Coef./(S.E.)* | *Coef./(S.E.)* | *Coef./(S.E.)* |
| Min. funding target | | | 0.001*** | 1.76e-06*** | | |
| | | | (0.0001) | (1.21e-07) | | |
| COVID period | 0.756 | −0.005 | 30.319 | −0.051 | −0.003 | 160.542 |
| | (1.03) | (0.10) | (37.12) | (0.08) | (0.04) | (98.38) |
| Interested investors | −0.001 | | | | | |
| | (0.002) | | | | | |
| Number of investors^ | | −3.06e-08** | 0.00002*** | – 1.34e-08 | 1.06e-10 | |
| | | (1.44e-08) | (5.94e-06) | (1.29e-08) | (6.33e-09) | |
| Percentage raised | | | 265.634*** | 0.828*** | 0.953*** | 341.916*** |
| | | | (34.72) | (0.08) | (0.04) | (56.96) |
| Percentage of capital raised^ | | | −19.650*** | −0.068*** | −0.072*** | |
| | | | (3.94) | (0.01) | (0.004) | |
| Capital raised§ | 9.461*** | 1.098*** | | | | −26.810 |
| | (2.17) | (0.08) | | | | (99.40) |
| Number of investors | 0.002 | 0.001*** | 0.162*** | 0.0001 | −0.00003 | |
| | (0.005) | (0.0001) | (0.06) | (0.0001) | (0.0001) | |
| Constant | −2.718 | 6.203*** | −542.150* | 11.034*** | −0.872* | −6620.045*** |
| | (12.75) | (1.04) | (310.80) | (0.68) | (0.47) | (1037.97) |
| *N* | 217 | 296 | 296 | 296 | 296 | 296 |

| | *(1) Campaign success* | *(2) Percentage raised* | *(3a) Capital raised (thousands)* | *(3b) Capital raised§* | *(3c) Capital raised§* | *(4) Number of investors* |
|---|---|---|---|---|---|---|
| | *Coef./(S.E.)* | *Coef./(S.E.)* | *Coef./(S.E.)* | *Coef./(S.E.)* | *Coef./(S.E.)* | *Coef./(S.E.)* |
| $R$-squared | | 0.76 | 0.93 | 0.79 | 0.95 | 0.46 |
| Pseudo $R^2$ | 0.60 | | | | | |
| AIC | 82.33 | 579.53 | 4101.88 | 471.68 | 72.15 | 4681.81 |
| BIC | 129.65 | 631.19 | 4157.23 | 527.03 | 127.50 | 4729.79 |

$^{*}p < 0.10$, $^{**}p < 0.05$, $^{***}p < 0.010$

**Table A.6** Multivariate analysis for Seedrs

| | *(1)* *Campaign success* *Coef./(S.E.)* | *(2)* *Percentage raised* *Coef./(S.E.)* | *(3a)* *Capital raised (thousands)* *Coef./(S.E.)* | *(3b)* *Capital raised§* *Coef./(S.E.)* | *(3c)* *Capital raised§* *Coef./(S.E.)* | *(4)* *Number of investors* *Coef./(S.E.)* |
|---|---|---|---|---|---|---|
| Equity retention | −0.033 | 0.013** | −440.445 | −0.385 | −0.382** | |
| | (0.05) | (0.01) | (330.82) | (0.26) | (0.16) | |
| Equity retention^ | | | 2.594 | 0.002 | 0.002** | |
| | | | (1.89) | (0.001) | (0.001) | |
| Social media count | 1.148* | 0.038 | −38.894 | −0.234** | 0.147** | 106.677** |
| | (0.64) | (0.07) | (148.03) | (0.12) | (0.07) | (44.34) |
| Share price§ | 0.108 | −0.040 | | | 0.070** | |
| | (0.19) | (0.03) | | | (0.03) | |
| Min. funding target | | | 0.002*** | 7.84e-07*** | | |
| | | | (0.0001) | (5.53e-08) | | |
| Min. funding target§ | −0.921* | −0.320*** | | | 0.936*** | 176.552*** |
| | (0.55) | (0.05) | | | (0.03) | (30.64) |
| COVID period | 0.165 | 0.023 | 216.130 | −0.200 | −0.132 | −49.558 |
| | (0.66) | (0.09) | (208.81) | (0.17) | (0.10) | (87.83) |
| Percentage raised | | | 877.694*** | 0.458*** | 0.398*** | |
| | | | (110.50) | (0.09) | (0.05) | |
| Share price | | | −0.014 | 0.00001 | | |
| | | | (0.07) | (0.0001) | | |

| | *(1)* *Campaign success* *Coef./(S.E.)* | *(2)* *Percentage raised* *Coef./(S.E.)* | *(3a)* *Capital raised (thousands)* *Coef./(S.E.)* | *(3b)* *Capital raised§* *Coef./(S.E.)* | *(3c)* *Capital raised§* *Coef./(S.E.)* | *(4)* *Number of investors* *Coef./(S.E.)* |
|---|---|---|---|---|---|---|
| Capital raised§ | 0.799 | 0.340*** | | | | |
| | (0.49) | (0.05) | | | | |
| Constant | 6.441 | −0.163 | 17,685.257 | 29.054** | 17.101** | −1894.375*** |
| | (5.43) | (0.67) | (14,404.03) | (11.47) | (6.90) | (389.85) |
| *N* | 366 | 366 | 366 | 366 | 366 | 80 |
| *R*-squared | | 0.16 | 0.62 | 0.39 | 0.78 | 0.33 |
| Pseudo $R^2$ | 0.03 | | | | | |
| AIC | 154.19 | 727.33 | 6377.61 | 1154.56 | 783.11 | 1132.07 |
| BIC | 181.51 | 754.65 | 6408.83 | 1185.78 | 814.33 | 1141.60 |

*$p < 0.10$, **$p < 0.05$, ***$p < 0.010$

**Table A.7** Multivariate analysis for Sowefund

| | *(1)* *Campaign success* *Coef./(Std. err.)* |
|---|---|
| Share price§ | 0.098 |
| | (0.19) |
| Min. funding target§ | 0.829** |
| | (0.40) |
| COVID period | −0.853 |
| | (0.83) |
| Constant | −11.551** |
| | (5.26) |
| *N* | 91 |
| *R*-squared | |
| Pseudo $R^2$ | 0.08 |
| AIC | 120.72 |
| BIC | 130.76 |

*$p$ < 0.10, **$p$ < 0.05, ***$p$ < 0.010

**Table A.8** Multivariate analysis for Companisto

| | *(3a)* *Capital raised (thousands)* *Coef./(Std. err.)* | *(3b)* *Capital raised§* *Coef./(Std. err.)* | *(3c)* *Capital raised§* *Coef./(Std. err.)* | *(4)* *Number of investors* *Coef./(Std. err.)* |
|---|---|---|---|---|
| COVID period | −30.741 | −0.068 | −0.054 | 13.837 |
| | (58.52) | (0.07) | (0.06) | (48.71) |
| Share price§ | | | 0.793** | |
| | | | (0.40) | |
| Share price§^ | | | 0.012 | |
| | | | (0.03) | |
| Share price | 0.701*** | 0.002*** | | −0.957*** |
| | (0.10) | (0.0001) | | (0.12) |
| Share price^ | 0.00004** | −3.05e-07*** | | 0.0001*** |
| | (0.00002) | (2.52e-08) | | (0.00003) |
| Capital raised (thousands) | | | | 1.456*** |
| | | | | (0.10) |
| Capital raised (thousands)^ | | | | −0.0002*** |
| | | | | (0.00003) |
| Number of investors | 0.239 | 0.004*** | 0.003*** | |
| | (0.16) | (0.0001) | (0.0001) | |
| Number of investors^ | 0.000*** | −9.69e-07*** | −8.86e-07*** | |
| | (0.00) | (9.61e-08) | (7.98e-08) | |
| Constant | −293.171*** | 9.735*** | 5.593*** | 568.286*** |
| | (76.06) | (0.09) | (1.24) | (40.10) |
| $N$ | 99 | 99 | 99 | 99 |
| $R$-squared | 0.91 | 0.94 | 0.96 | 0.83 |
| Pseudo $R^2$ | | | | |
| AIC | 1340.68 | 13.03 | −22.86 | 1304.07 |
| BIC | 1356.25 | 28.60 | −7.29 | 1319.64 |

*$p < 0.10$, **$p < 0.05$, ***$p < 0.010$

**Table A.9** Multivariate analysis for FundedByMe

| | *(3a)* *Capital raised (thousands)* *Coef./(Std. err.)* | *(3b)* *Capital raised§* *Coef./(Std. err.)* |
|---|---|---|
| Equity retention | −11.568*** | −0.036*** |
| | (2.88) | (0.01) |
| Social media presence | 105.266* | 0.522*** |
| | (58.43) | (0.19) |
| Firm location | 26.847 | −0.089 |
| | (53.83) | (0.18) |
| COVID period | 36.707 | 0.151 |
| | (62.37) | (0.21) |
| Constant | 1184.249*** | 14.682*** |
| | (266.63) | (0.89) |
| $N$ | 184 | 184 |
| $R$-squared | 0.10 | 0.10 |
| Pseudo $R^2$ | | |
| AIC | 2648.45 | 548.20 |
| BIC | 2664.52 | 564.27 |

*$p < 0.10$, **$p < 0.05$, ***$p < 0.010$

**Table A.10** Multivariate analysis for Invesdor

| | *(1)* *Campaign success* *Coef./(Std. err.)* | *(2)* *Percentage raised* *Coef./(Std. err.)* | *(3a)* *Capital raised (thousands)* *Coef./(Std. err.)* | *(3b)* *Capital raised§* *Coef./(Std. err.)* | *(3c)* *Capital raised§* *Coef./(Std. err.)* |
|---|---|---|---|---|---|
| Entrepreneur gender | 0.395 | −0.419* | 155.053 | 0.237* | 0.199** |
| | (1.13) | (0.23) | (103.60) | (0.14) | (0.08) |
| Social media presence | −2.366 | −0.166 | 127.137 | 0.227* | −0.031 |
| | (1.79) | (0.22) | (101.88) | (0.13) | (0.07) |
| Firm location | | 0.548* | | | |
| | | (0.32) | | | |
| Financial forecast | −1.26e-06*** | | −1.04e-06 | 6.98e-09 | |
| | (4.58e-07) | | (7.35e-06) | (9.72e-09) | |
| Financial forecast^ | 3.80e-14** | | | | |
| | (1.89e-14) | | | | |
| Financial forecast§ | | 0.071 | | | 0.022 |
| | | (0.09) | | | (0.03) |
| Financial forecast (year) = 2015 | | 0.000 | 0.000 | 0.000 | 0.000 |
| | | (.) | (.) | (.) | (.) |
| Financial forecast (year) = 2016 | | 0.235 | 65.688 | 0.141 | 0.123 |
| | | (0.33) | (146.08) | (0.19) | (0.12) |
| Financial forecast (year) = 2017 | | 0.182 | 98.278 | 0.559*** | 0.002 |
| | | (0.37) | (157.30) | (0.21) | (0.13) |
| Financial forecast (year) = 2018 | | 0.051 | 271.856* | 0.662*** | 0.068 |

(continued)

**Table A.10** (continued)

| | *(1)* *Campaign success* *Coef./(Std. err.)* | *(2)* *Percentage raised* *Coef./(Std. err.)* | *(3a)* *Capital raised (thousands)* *Coef./(Std. err.)* | *(3b)* *Capital raised§* *Coef./(Std. err.)* | *(3c)* *Capital raised§* *Coef./(Std. err.)* |
|---|---|---|---|---|---|
| | | (0.34) | (139.20) | (0.18) | (0.12) |
| Financial forecast (year) = 2019 | | 0.260 | 17.657 | 0.361* | −0.124 |
| | | (0.38) | (162.30) | (0.21) | (0.13) |
| Financial forecast (year) = 2020 | | 0.344 | 123.714 | 0.476** | −0.197 |
| | | (0.40) | (166.09) | (0.22) | (0.14) |
| Min. funding target§ | | −1.708*** | | | 0.987*** |
| | | (0.19) | | | (0.05) |
| Min. funding target | | | 0.002*** | 2.65e-06*** | |
| | | | (0.0001) | (2.47e-07) | |
| Outstanding shares§ | | | | | 0.020 |
| | | | | | (0.02) |
| Outstanding shares | 1.36e-07 | −2.83e-09 | 7.21e-06 | 6.08e-09 | |
| | (2.32e-07) | (1.54e-08) | (6.88e-06) | (9.10e-09) | |
| COVID period | −0.876 | 0.143 | −208.722** | −0.176 | −0.087 |
| | (1.04) | (0.23) | (100.55) | (0.13) | (0.08) |
| Percentage raised | | | 447.589*** | 0.822*** | 0.909*** |
| | | | (75.97) | (0.10) | (0.06) |
| Percentage of capital raised^ | | | −29.837*** | −0.052*** | −0.065*** |
| | | | (8.70) | (0.01) | (0.01) |

| | *(1)* *Campaign success* *Coef./(Std. err.)* | *(2)* *Percentage raised* *Coef./(Std. err.)* | *(3a)* *Capital raised (thousands)* *Coef./(Std. err.)* | *(3b)* *Capital raised§* *Coef./(Std. err.)* | *(3c)* *Capital raised§* *Coef./(Std. err.)* |
|---|---|---|---|---|---|
| Capital raised§ | 2.504*** | 1.597*** | | | |
| | (0.77) | (0.14) | | | |
| Constant | −22.572*** | 0.991 | −806.470*** | 9.990*** | −1.278** |
| | (7.86) | (1.57) | (172.35) | (0.23) | (0.54) |
| *N* | 92 | 92 | 92 | 92 | 92 |
| *R*-squared | | 0.68 | 0.72 | 0.83 | 0.94 |
| Pseudo $R^2$ | 0.46 | | | | |
| AIC | 46.80 | 240.64 | 1363.52 | 143.84 | 44.97 |
| BIC | 64.45 | 275.94 | 1398.82 | 179.14 | 80.28 |

*$p < 0.10$, **$p < 0.05$, ***$p < 0.010$

**Table A.11** Multivariate analysis for 200Crowd

| | *(1) Campaign success Coef./(Std. err.)* | *(2) Percentage raised Coef./(Std. err.)* | *(3a) Capital raised (thousands) Coef./(Std. err.)* | *(3b) Capital raised§ Coef./(Std. err.)* | *(3c) Capital raised§ Coef./(Std. err.)* | *(4) Number of investors Coef./(Std. err.)* | *(5) Professional investor Coef./(Std. err.)* |
|---|---|---|---|---|---|---|---|
| Equity retention | | −0.064*** | −4.073 | 0.0004 | 0.017 | 1.631* | −0.869 |
| | | (0.02) | (4.44) | (0.02) | (0.02) | (0.94) | (0.58) |
| Pre-money | | | 0.00001 | 2.08e-08 | | | |
| | | | (0.00001) | (6.64e-08) | | | |
| Pre-money§ | −1.663 | 0.539*** | | | −0.165 | −9.452 | 0.772 |
| | (1.47) | (0.16) | | | (0.22) | (8.80) | (2.23) |
| Min. funding target | | | 0.001*** | 4.75e-06*** | | | |
| | | | (0.0002) | (1.44e-06) | | | |
| Min. funding target§ | −0.734 | −1.036*** | | | 1.094*** | 21.091* | −1.620 |
| | (1.58) | (0.18) | | | (0.25) | (11.66) | (3.07) |
| COVID period | 2.734 | −0.049 | −11.653 | 0.115 | −0.048 | 4.956 | |
| | (9.94) | (0.20) | (50.43) | (0.26) | (0.24) | (9.55) | |
| Interested investors | −0.223 | −0.008* | 0.597 | 0.009 | 0.009 | 1.376*** | 0.017 |
| | (0.17) | (0.004) | (1.25) | (0.01) | (0.01) | (0.04) | (0.08) |
| Capital raised§ | | 0.422*** | | | | −6.792 | −0.182 |
| | | (0.11) | | | | (6.17) | (2.24) |
| Percentage raised | | | 154.399*** | 0.561*** | 0.636*** | 22.490*** | 6.017 |

| | (1) Campaign success Coef./(Std. err.) | (2) Percentage raised Coef./(Std. err.) | (3a) Capital raised (thousands) Coef./(Std. err.) | (3b) Capital raised§ Coef./(Std. err.) | (3c) Capital raised§ Coef./(Std. err.) | (4) Number of investors Coef./(Std. err.) | (5) Professional investor Coef./(Std. err.) |
|---|---|---|---|---|---|---|---|
| | | | (35.78) | (0.18) | (0.17) | (6.65) | (4.75) |
| Number of investors | 0.558* | 0.013*** | −0.695 | 0.0003 | −0.0005 | | −0.022 |
| | (0.30) | (0.003) | (0.99) | (0.01) | (0.004) | | (0.06) |
| Number of investors^ | | −5.45e-06* | 0.001* | −8.65e-06** | −5.46e-06 | | |
| | | (2.72e-06) | (0.0007) | (3.80e-06) | (3.40e-06) | | |
| Professional investor | | 0.090 | 11.370 | 1.177*** | 1.133*** | 10.973 | |
| | | (0.27) | (58.05) | (0.30) | (0.28) | (12.39) | |
| Constant | 27.606 | 6.297*** | 140.928 | 8.920*** | −2.288 | −213.846* | 87.408 |
| | (18.23) | (2.12) | (434.26) | (2.22) | (2.86) | (108.21) | (56.25) |
| *N* | 48 | 48 | 48 | 48 | 48 | 48 | 48 |
| *R*-squared | | 0.86 | 0.95 | 0.83 | 0.85 | 0.98 | |
| Pseudo $R^2$ | 0.79 | | | | | | 0.82 |
| AIC | 22.08 | 71.57 | 604.10 | 97.59 | 91.21 | 444.41 | 28.30 |
| BIC | 33.31 | 90.28 | 622.82 | 116.30 | 109.92 | 461.25 | 43.27 |

$^*p < 0.10$, $^{**}p < 0.05$, $^{***}p < 0.010$

**Table A.12** Multivariate analysis for Mamacrowd

| | *(2) Percentage raised* | *(3a) Capital raised (thousands)* | *(3b) Capital raised§* | *(3c) Capital raised§* | *(4) Number of investors* | *(5) Professional investor* |
|---|---|---|---|---|---|---|
| | *Coef./(Std. err.)* | *Coef./(Std. err.)* | *Coef./(Std. err.)* | *Coef./(Std. err.)* | *Coef./(Std. err.)* | *Coef./(Std. err.)* |
| Entrepreneur gender | 0.505 | 64.413 | 0.034 | −0.040 | −21.010 | −1.523 |
| | (0.35) | (86.98) | (0.92) | (0.94) | (55.68) | (10.54) |
| Equity retention | 0.011 | 2.324 | −0.027 | −0.030 | 0.219 | 0.675 |
| | (0.01) | (2.40) | (0.03) | (0.03) | (1.73) | (0.64) |
| Social media presence | −0.303 | −405.319*** | −3.159** | −2.348* | 5.412 | 5.499 |
| | (0.52) | (125.60) | (1.33) | (1.36) | (81.16) | (18.90) |
| Social media count | −0.201 | −30.760 | −1.041** | −0.960** | 71.804*** | −4.835 |
| | (0.16) | (38.66) | (0.41) | (0.41) | (24.75) | (4.52) |
| Equity§ | −0.041 | | | −0.040 | −9.209 | |
| | (0.07) | | | (0.18) | (10.47) | |
| Pre-money§ | 1.258 | | | 0.347 | −220.407* | −9.854 |
| | (0.86) | | | (0.28) | (131.50) | (8.62) |
| Pre-money^ | −0.054 | | | | 9.712* | |
| | (0.04) | | | | (5.45) | |
| Pre-money valuation | | 9.73e-06 | 2.51e-07* | | | |
| | | (.00001) | (1.37e-07) | | | |
| Min. funding target | | 0.0003 | 4.37e-07 | | | |
| | | (0.0003) | (3.51e-06) | | | |

| | (2) *Percentage raised* *Coef./(Std. err.)* | (3a) *Capital raised (thousands)* *Coef./(Std. err.)* | (3b) *Capital raised§* *Coef./(Std. err.)* | (3c) *Capital raised§* *Coef./(Std. err.)* | (4) *Number of investors* *Coef./(Std. err.)* | (5) *Professional investor* *Coef./(Std. err.)* |
|---|---|---|---|---|---|---|
| Maximum investment target | | 0.00004 | 4.28e-07 | | | |
| | | (0.00004) | (4.45e-07) | | | |
| Share price | | 0.006 | −0.0001 | | | |
| | | (0.01) | (0.0001) | | | |
| Share price§ | 0.368** | | | −0.166 | −308.970 | |
| | (0.17) | | | (0.46) | (207.76) | |
| Share price^ | | | | | 18.833 | |
| | | | | | (14.83) | |
| Equity | | −0.0001** | −1.64e-06** | | | |
| | | (0.00006) | (6.23e-07) | | | |
| Min. funding target§ | −0.684*** | | | 0.083 | 56.231 | −2.550 |
| | (0.23) | | | (0.62) | (36.88) | (4.90) |
| Max. funding target§ | 11.955*** | | | 1.313** | −2113.954*** | |
| | (3.64) | | | (0.60) | (557.43) | |
| Max. funding target^ | −0.447*** | | | | 81.131*** | |

(continued)

**Table A.12** (continued)

| | *(2) Percentage raised* <br> *Coef./(Std. err.)* | *(3a) Capital raised (thousands)* <br> *Coef./(Std. err.)* | *(3b) Capital raised§* <br> *Coef./(Std. err.)* | *(3c) Capital raised§* <br> *Coef./(Std. err.)* | *(4) Number of investors* <br> *Coef./(Std. err.)* | *(5) Professional investor* <br> *Coef./(Std. err.)* |
|---|---|---|---|---|---|---|
| | (0.14) | | | | (20.77) | |
| COVID period | 0.352 | 155.293* | 1.657* | 1.338 | −52.609 | 0.862 |
| | (0.35) | (87.13) | (0.92) | (0.91) | (55.13) | (4.20) |
| Percentage raised | | −44.001 | −0.012 | 0.117 | 57.200*** | |
| | | (27.37) | (0.29) | (0.28) | (12.72) | |
| Capital raised§ | 0.011 | | | | 9.773 | −0.232 |
| | (0.04) | | | | (6.47) | (0.61) |
| Number of investors | 0.014*** | 2.656*** | 0.013** | 0.008 | | 0.385 |
| | (0.001) | (0.54) | (0.01) | (0.01) | | (0.26) |
| Number of investors^ | −5.17e-06*** | −0.001*** | −4.47e-06* | −2.60e-06 | | |
| | (8.00e-07) | (0.0002) | (2.47e-06) | (2.50e-06) | | |
| Professional investor | 0.763** | −13.306 | 1.493 | 1.452 | −39.801 | |
| | (0.37) | (89.94) | (0.95) | (0.97) | (57.92) | |
| Constant | −80.565*** | 100.193 | 11.060*** | −10.155 | 15,256.336*** | 110.129 |
| | (26.14) | (244.82) | (2.59) | (8.60) | (3890.60) | (85.71) |
| *N* | 97 | 97 | 97 | 97 | 97 | 97 |

| | (2) *Percentage raised* *Coef./(Std. err.)* | (3a) *Capital raised (thousands)* *Coef./(Std. err.)* | (3b) *Capital raised§* *Coef./(Std. err.)* | (3c) *Capital raised§* *Coef./(Std. err.)* | (4) *Number of investors* *Coef./(Std. err.)* | (5) *Professional investor* *Coef./(Std. err.)* |
|---|---|---|---|---|---|---|
| *R*-squared | 0.69 | 0.73 | 0.58 | 0.56 | 0.57 | |
| Pseudo $R^2$ | | | | | | 0.86 |
| AIC | 298.52 | 1363.58 | 481.16 | 484.97 | 1279.40 | 29.69 |
| BIC | 342.29 | 1402.20 | 519.78 | 523.59 | 1323.17 | 55.44 |

$^{*}p < 0.10$, $^{**}p < 0.05$, $^{***}p < 0.010$

**Table A.13** Multivariate analysis for Opstart

| | (1) *Campaign success* *Coef./(Std. err.)* | (3a) *Capital raised (thousands)* *Coef./(Std. err.)* | (3b) *Capital raised§* *Coef./(Std. err.)* | (3c) *Capital raised§* *Coef./(Std. err.)* |
|---|---|---|---|---|
| Entrepreneur gender | −0.407 | −4.686 | −0.731 | −0.620 |
| | (1.53) | (165.81) | (0.51) | (0.51) |
| Social media count | 0.141 | −7.675 | 0.048 | 0.064 |
| | (0.57) | (63.05) | (0.19) | (0.19) |
| Pre-money | | 1.30e-06 | 1.57e-07* | |
| | | (0.00002) | (8.60e-08) | |
| Pre-money§ | 0.808 | | | 0.091 |
| | (0.63) | | | (0.13) |
| Min. funding target§ | −1.204 | | | |
| | (0.85) | | | |
| Min. funding target | | −0.001 | 1.36e-06 | −6.93e-07 |
| | | (0.001) | (3.23e-06) | (3.42e-06) |
| Min. funding target^ | | 2.49e-09 | 4.53e-13 | 5.28e-12 |
| | | (1.63e-09) | (4.97e-12) | (4.76e-12) |
| Max. funding target§ | −2.469* | | | −11.733* |
| | (1.44) | | | (6.17) |
| Max. funding target | | 0.002 | 0.00001** | |
| | | (0.002) | (5.53e-06) | |
| Max. retail investment | | 0.002 | 0.000132 | 12.121* |
| | | (0.002) | (5.77e-06) | (6.11) |
| Max. retail investment§ | 4.40e-06 | | | 12.121* |
| | (3.20e-06) | | | (6.11) |
| COVID period | −1.632** | −121.452 | −0.520* | −0.586* |
| | (0.79) | (102.12) | (0.31) | (0.30) |
| Share price | | 0.015* | 0.00001 | |
| | | (0.01) | (0.00002) | |

| | *(1)* *Campaign success* *Coef./(Std. err.)* | *(3a)* *Capital raised (thousands)* *Coef./(Std. err.)* | *(3b)* *Capital raised§* *Coef./(Std. err.)* | *(3c)* *Capital raised§* *Coef./(Std. err.)* |
|---|---|---|---|---|
| Share price§ | 1.503 | | | 0.215** |
| | (1.19) | | | (0.10) |
| Constant | 25.233 | 91.033 | 11.147*** | 4.988** |
| | (17.73) | (101.15) | (0.31) | (2.47) |
| $N$ | 79 | 78 | 78 | 79 |
| $R$-squared | | 0.83 | 0.40 | 0.40 |
| Pseudo $R^2$ | 0.20 | | | |
| AIC | 67.73 | 1138.87 | 233.08 | 235.15 |
| BIC | 89.05 | 1162.44 | 254.29 | 256.47 |

*$p < 0.10$, **$p < 0.05$, ***$p < 0.010$

# Index






F. J. Mazzocchini and C. Lucarelli, *Investors' Preferences in Financing New Ventures*,
https://doi.org/10.1007/978-3-031-30058-5

GPSR Compliance
The European Union's (EU) General Product Safety Regulation (GPSR) is a set of rules that requires consumer products to be safe and our obligations to ensure this.

If you have any concerns about our products, you can contact us on

ProductSafety@springernature.com

In case Publisher is established outside the EU, the EU authorized representative is:

Springer Nature Customer Service Center GmbH
Europaplatz 3
69115 Heidelberg, Germany

www.ingramcontent.com/pod-product-compliance
Ingram Content Group UK Ltd.
Pitfield, Milton Keynes, MK11 3LW, UK
UKHW020836290926
15470UKWH00004B/1386
* 9 7 8 3 0 3 1 3 0 0 5 7 8 *